AN APPLE A DAY

A Memoir of Love and Recovery From Anorexia

Emma Woolf

SOFT SKULL PRESS
An imprint of COUNTERPOINT
BERKELEY

Library of Congress Cataloging-in-Publication data is available
ISBN 978-1-59376-515-6

Cover design by Gerilyn Attebery
Interior design by Emma Cofod

SOFT SKULL PRESS
An imprint of COUNTERPOINT
1919 Fifth Street
Berkeley, CA 94710
www.softskull.com
www.counterpointpress.com

Printed in the United States of America
Distributed by Publishers Group West

10 9 8 7 6 5 4 3 2 1

To Tom

About the Author

Photograph by Thomas Skovsende

EMMA WOOLF is the great-niece of Virginia Woolf. She studied at Oxford University and worked in publishing before becoming a freelance journalist and writer, contributing to *The Independent, Harper's Bazaar, Red, Grazia, The Times,* and *The Mail on Sunday.* She lives in London. You can follow Emma on Twitter: @ejwoolf.

Contents

AN APPLE A DAY

Introduction

Everything is white, silent and cold. I haven't tasted chocolate for over ten years and now I'm walking down the street unwrapping a Kit Kat. I don't know which is stranger—this sudden fall of snow, blanketing London in stillness, or eating a bar of chocolate in public. It tastes amazing.

This moment may sound mundane but it represents a new food frontier for me. It's a target I've set myself and it's taken me weeks to find the courage. This morning I woke early and knew it was time. So I bought a large coffee and the chocolate bar and walked alone in the snow, savoring every warm, melting mouthful.

How long is it exactly since I last ate chocolate? Put it this way: the last Kit Kat I bought was in paper and silver foil, not this hermetically sealed wrapper. After an absence of more than a decade, it's clear that the world of chocolate has expanded—there are so many varieties on offer: mint and orange flavors, limited-edition peanut and caramel, even "chunky" versions.

Remember when Kate Moss said, "Nothing tastes as good as skinny feels"? She's wrong: chocolate does.

As I walk and eat and sip, I reflect on the challenge I set myself a few months back, in autumn, and the progress I've made. Even though it's nearly Christmas and I haven't bought a single present yet, I feel a weird sense of optimism. As this year draws to a close I have decided to put a lot of neuroses and regrets and sadness behind me; everybody gets hurt and makes mistakes, but life goes on. I have to get some extra weight under my belt; I want to make next year the year that everything changes. I'm going to stop looking back or worrying about the future.

There's no point dwelling on the past, but you can learn from it. Here are a few food-and-love-related lessons I've learned in the past few months:

Lesson 1: It's exciting to go outside your safety zone and try new foods. Who knew that Marks & Spencer Super Wholefood Couscous would be so tasty?

Lesson 2: Being healthy and happy are more important than your salary or career.

Lesson 3: Loving someone else is fairly easy; it's allowing yourself to be fully loved that is hard.

Lesson 4: Fat is not the enemy: olive oil, hummus, and Brazil nuts give you shiny hair, not a fat bum.

As this year ends I've been looking back and looking forward. But why do we make New Year's resolutions? Why should the coldest, darkest month of the year be a good time for change? I don't know, but something about the year ahead feels hopeful. For Christmas I'm giving myself a fresh start. This year I'm going to kick down my barriers and let Tom love me and take more risks.

Maybe it's as simple as this: I'm bored of anorexia. It's exhausting to fight yourself every minute of every day, and I'm tired of waging this one-woman battle against myself. I want to move on with my life; I want to have a baby. I'm bored of the anorexia trap.

As Tom is always telling me, "If you just let go a little, life could be so sweet." I know he's right. It's time to let go.

So, here's to letting go. This morning I received a handwritten letter from a woman who suffered from anorexia for fifty years.

Everyone had told me I was too old for treatment but eventually I was referred to a young psychiatrist. Of course I had no faith in him and only continued because he didn't seem to mind me wasting his time. But to my amazement, after a while, it began to work . . . It took a lot of time and hard work, but we've managed to achieve something that to me still seems nothing less than a miracle. At seventy-four years old, I can now eat perfectly normally—anything I want. I cannot describe the happiness of knowing that I am free to enjoy however many years I have left.

Which just goes to show—it's never too late to start again.

* * *

But how did I reach this point? How did I get to the stage where I hadn't eaten chocolate for ten years? Why was it such an ordeal to eat in public? What had happened to make me so terrified of food? How had I caught this disease we call anorexia . . . and how was I ever going to recover?

There are lots of questions and many different answers. For me it's been too long in this fight, and the only answer I want right now is the one about recovery: is it possible to beat anorexia, and will I be able to do it? After years of thinking about this and trying different strategies, I haven't found a solution. It's quite a struggle, I do know that.

* * *

I don't really know how it started. A diet that got out of control, a broken heart, perfectionism and shaky body image, faulty brain chemistry, pressure from society or the media or me? Probably all those reasons and others too—many of which I'm still trying to work out as I write. There's never a single reason: the causes of anorexia are numerous, complex, and highly individual. What matters now is not how it started but how it ends.

Let me explain: I have an eating disorder and I can function fine on an apple a day. But it's been ten years and I'm starting to see that it's not fine at all. So, three months ago at the start of autumn, I set myself a challenge—the biggest challenge of my life: I decided that over the next year I'm going to overcome anorexia. I'm going to stop living on fruit and yogurt, and start eating normal food, like a normal person, in a normal way. I'm going to reach a healthy weight so that I'm fertile again. (I'm not going to freak out when my period returns, I'm going to celebrate.) I'm not going to starve myself anymore; I'm going to be an adult and feed myself. I'm going to shop and cook and eat with the rest of the world. I'm going to find something even more addictive and compelling than hunger. I'm going to rejoin the human race; I'm going to take part.

Fact number 1: I've just turned thirty-three.

Fact number 2: I've wasted my twenties not recovering from anorexia. I will not waste my thirties.

Fact number 3: All the therapy and drugs in the world won't cure you of anorexia. Over the years I've tried everything: counseling, psychoanalysis, medication, homeopathy, acupuncture. I've made countless promises to myself and others, and each time I've failed. There is no magic bullet. To beat anorexia you have to eat.

Fact number 4: It's not about appearance. I don't think the skeletal look is remotely attractive.

So what's it all about? I don't know, really . . . It's an addiction and a compulsion, a brain disorder and a crutch, your best friend and your worst enemy, a fight between body and soul. Anorexia is an illness that takes on a life of its own, feeding on itself as you starve. It's a voice in your head that never, *ever* shuts up.

Just to clarify: I'm not *sick*-sick anymore. My low point, age twenty-one, was 77 pounds (I'm now around 105 pounds). I find it upsetting now to recall my lowest weight: I don't know how that fragile girl stayed alive every day. I remember that I was cold all the time, because I had no subcutaneous fat. The body finds it very hard to function without this natural thermal layer, without caloric heat or energy going in; as any anorexic will tell you, winter is terrifying. I remember that lots of things hurt: lying down at night was painful because my bones had no cushioning against the mattress; sitting down was painful because my tail bone dug into the chair; I was covered in bruises from the slightest knock.

But that was then, that was over ten years ago . . . Somehow I stayed out of the hospital and got through my Oxford finals and got myself out of the danger zone. I've had a good career in publishing and journalism ever since. I bought my own flat in a trendy part of North London with not-too-noisy neighbors. I have a crazy but loving family—two brothers, two sisters, two parents, and an ever-expanding troop of nephews and nieces. Two years ago I met Tom, my boyfriend (of whom I'll say much more later).

But here's the thing: I never actually got better. I put on some weight—enough that I don't get stared at in the street these days, enough that lying in bed isn't painful anymore—but I never found a cure for the illness in my head. Anorexia is such a visible condition, and people focus relentlessly on the body shape and weight of the sufferer. This leads to the common misconception that anorexia is about looking good—that sufferers are losing weight in order to attain the perfect body.

What bullshit. There's nothing less attractive than wasting away; no anorexic thinks they actually look sexy. You avoid interaction with others, and you fear human contact. You don't have the slightest desire for sex, or even for flirting, and you certainly don't want to flaunt your scrawny body. When you're staying alive on almost zero food you have no energy left over for the outside world, for fun or sex. I won't pretend that I didn't have sexual relationships when I was at my thinnest—I did, and anorexics do—but the feel-good hormones aren't really there. It's hard enough just thinking straight when you have so little fuel.

To me, the focus on body shape is misguided. For such a physical illness, anorexia has surprisingly little to do with external appearance. Of course it usually starts out that way, as a normal diet, but it quickly transmutes into an internal sickness. My experience of anorexia is of a profound disconnect between my body and my mind. The more weight I lost, the more I retreated into myself; I became a human husk, cold and isolated. I felt so brittle I avoided hugs.

My rock bottom: dropping below 85 pounds. Everything began to shut down. Oxford is "on the clay," which means it gets extremely cold in winter. The only thing that still functioned was my brain, just about, so I concentrated on my university degree. I spent hours in the Upper Reading Room of the Bodleian Library memorizing vast chunks of the Old English set texts. When the outside world got to be too much, I locked myself in my college room writing essays on the metaphysical poets. I knew I had to focus on reading and writing and passing my finals before I lost my mental faculties too.

Friends at university were worried and they talked, first to my face and then behind my back. Call it defensiveness or pride, but I've always detested pity. I hate the feeling that people are "concerned" about me: I'd rather be bitched about than pitied. But what do you say to someone who is fading away? Yes, I went to see doctors. I only had to step on the scale for them to make the diagnosis. As a teenager, I'd always been an average height and weight—at five foot six I weighed between 125 and 135 pounds. So, by dropping to 85 pounds and then lower, I more than fulfilled the strict medical criterion for anorexia: the loss of a third of your body weight.

In the end I just wanted everyone to leave me alone.

Anorexia is a frightening word. Of course I'd known I was sick long before any health professional used the term—I felt myself spiraling downward, my body in free fall. What had started as a diet got way out of control. Quite quickly I found I was struggling to eat anything at all. I would cut out certain food groups (all fats), then cut out specific foods, and then find ways to cut out more. (There never was a plateau, weirdly: even at the lowest food intake it always seemed possible to reduce it further.) Every time I put on my Levi's they were looser. I was losing weight at a rate of knots. I knew I was in serious trouble, sure. But it's a shock, nonetheless; something like the first time you hear the word "cancer," or even "alcoholic."

On a personal level, let me tell you what the repeated use of that label does. It makes you sicker; it traps you in the condition. They have defined you as an anorexic, so you must be thin, right? From that point on, whenever you eat (even if it's just raw carrots) you feel like a fraud. If you were a proper anorexic, you wouldn't eat, that's what the voice inside your head tells you.

And even when you're getting better, the label is misleading: when you put on weight, you will be cured, right? The key to beating anorexia is to gain weight, isn't it? Wrong, wrong, wrong. The illness is in my head, not on the scale or in the size of my body.

Throughout this book, whenever I refer to weight—whether I've gained or lost—how much we're all supposed to weigh, a normal or abnormal body mass index (BMI), please remember this: anorexia is a mental illness. Gaining weight is the physical cure, of course, but it doesn't deal with the sickness.

Don't believe me? I know a woman who is 266 pounds who still has anorexia. She has gained the weight back (and more), and this means that on strict medical criterion she is no longer defined as anorexic. But that's precisely the point. Mentally, she has never recovered from the disease.

* * *

More than ten years on from those skeletal Oxford days, I now have the confidence to say that I haven't recovered either. I've remained underweight, hovering in the twilight zone. I look normal, but I haven't had my period for over a decade. (Writing that shocks me.)

The problem with this kind of "functional" anorexia is that you can carry on forever—there's no talk of emergency measures, no hospitalization or force-feeding. You seem OK, just thin. The recent vogue for "managed anorexia" is alarming: managed anorexics are normal women, with careers, children, normal lives, who admit to being constantly, obsessively vigilant about what they eat in order to remain thin. The discussion of managed anorexia is often humorous in tone, flippant even, but there's nothing funny about semi-starvation. I believe that a lot of women are living like this, hungry all the time.

And at this level, just hovering in the underweight category on the BMI charts, the health risks are mostly invisible—amenorrhoea (loss of periods), infertility, depression, insomnia, and osteopenia (the precursor to osteoporosis, severe loss of bone density). You can't see these things from the outside. No big deal, no crisis.

But of course it's a crisis, I know that. Every day that goes by now is another day wasted.

In the end it's about change, the paralyzing fear of change. Anorexia keeps you frozen in its icy grip. The notion that life could be any different—that it could be better—becomes inconceivable. You forget how good it was to be normal. Worst of all, you come to believe you prefer it this way. I've been trapped for too long. It's time to stop the madness.

* * *

So why now? It began in the autumn, after a conversation with my boyfriend, Tom, when he said, "There's one more thing I want you to promise me." He looked more serious than I'd ever seen him. "You have to stop running. And if we're serious about having a baby, you have to eat more." Stop running *and* start eating, was he kidding? What did he think I was, Wonder Woman? Running is my lifesaver, my natural Prozac; it's the addiction that replaced cigarettes five years ago.

We were sitting in Starbucks in St. Katharine Docks (the best Starbucks in London with its Palladian dome and secret top floor). The place was packed with secretaries and business men in suits, holding work meetings or catching up on gossip. We were tucked away at our favorite table in the corner. Stop running? I eyed my boyfriend skeptically over the rim of my grande decaf black Americano.

"I mean it, Em, you're going to have to cut out the running. You've been avoiding this for way too long." He looked at me and I looked back and neither of us said a word. This was an ultimatum of sorts, we both knew that.

And Tom wasn't telling me anything new: I've known for years that my lifestyle is unsustainable. Getting up at 6 AM and running four or five miles on nothing but a double espresso, burning up fuel (and fat and muscle) that I simply don't have to spare. I was out there pounding the pavement every morning without fail, rain or shine; I was running myself into the ground. I could carry on that way forever, but there'd be no chance of having a baby. Yes, I understood that.

Tom reached across and took my hand, softening the tension in the air. "I know you can do this, Em, your body needs a break. And as well as cutting out the running, you're going to have to start eating properly. Eating isn't greedy—it's fuel; it's about our plans and dreams, making all that possible. It's you taking the decision to get your health back, simple as that."

We'd had this conversation many times before—sometimes in anger, sometimes in sadness or despair—but that time it was different. That day we talked about the future with a new seriousness, all the happy things that could be waiting around the corner (a baby among them) if only I could get myself unstuck. It's a question of gaining 10 or 20 pounds, according to my doctors. So little and yet so much.

In addition to control and food and body image and all the other issues in eating disorders, there's a huge degree of self-deceit. It's not rocket science and I know it: I haven't recovered because I haven't wanted it *enough*.

And here's the thing: time runs out. Remember your twenties? Didn't you feel like you were invincible? I had serious boyfriends, but I didn't seriously want to have children back then. I was too busy building my career, and buying my first flat, and generally finding out who I was . . . it was never the right time or place for children.

But sitting in Starbucks that autumn day, I felt differently. Looking across at Tom, thinking about our future, our baby, making a home, a family together, I realized now I wanted all that more than I wanted to be thin. When I think of the wasted years, the evenings spent alone, the friends lost, the conviviality and enjoyment of eating with others, all those shared meals I've avoided . . . it strikes me as incredibly sad. I'll never get those years back. Anorexia is a young person's game and I don't have the time or energy to play anymore.

I knew Tom was right; I knew something had to change. People have told me I have an iron will, resisting food, starving myself into oblivion and all that . . . but I didn't know if I had the will-power for this.

That was the hardest and most honest conversation Tom and I had ever had. I agreed to stop running and start eating. We finished our coffees and walked along the docks and kissed goodbye; Tom went back to his office and I went off to find my bike.

Cycling back through the city, around the Barbican and up to Angel, I was filled with hope and fear. The wind in my hair, the first chill of autumn in the air, the promise of a new start. I stopped at Sainsbury's and bought a large pot of natural organic probiotic yogurt *with fat*. Not much fat (and admittedly I dithered in front of the freezer for half an hour) but it was a huge step for a fat-phobic food dodger like me.

Eyeing my running shoes later that evening, I realized this was going to be bloody hard to put into practice. Waking up and not running? Waking up and eating instead? How do other people do it?

* * *

It's been eleven weeks since that conversation with Tom in Starbucks—exactly eleven weeks since my last run. Of course I'm still procrastinating: sitting here typing about recovery, all words and no action. Yes, I've stopped running. That was the promise I made and I miss it every morning. I'm convinced I've lost muscle tone, but I keep telling myself it's a small price to pay to get my life back. Not running is the strongest thing I've done in ages. But what about eating?

Well, I'm having limited success. Eating is something I find unaccountably, inexplicably complicated. It feels greedy. I worry that if I start, I'll never be able to stop. And anyway, I don't think I deserve to eat.

Recovery from anorexia is hard, because it involves a whole new way of thinking. Tom compares it to giving up smoking or cutting back on booze, but that's not quite right. I gave up smoking, I can go weeks without drinking, but *starting* to eat is a different challenge altogether. Getting through the withdrawal of nicotine was tough, no doubt about it, but it was all about willpower. And there were immediate benefits to kicking the habit: I found I could run faster, for longer; I could breathe more easily; my skin looked clearer, fresher. With eating, for a recovering anorexic, there seem to be no rewards: all that will happen, for a certainty, is that you will gain weight. And that's the thing you dread above all else.

Nevertheless, I made the commitment: I will start eating.

* * *

First, I want to set out what politicians call their *red lines*. As with the rest of my life there will be rules. There are things I will try to do differently and other things I can't change. Most obviously, being a vegetarian . . . I'm not going to start eating meat or fish or anything living. I won't willingly add fat to food—I don't want butter on my bread—and I won't eat rich, creamy sauces. I will accept some essential fats—balsamic vinegar and olive oil on salads for example—although I can't see myself eating handfuls of nuts. I will drink semi-skimmed milk, not skimmed. I will not feel guilty for eating bread and pasta or other carbohydrates. I will eat in public, if I have to; I will try to eat unscheduled food once in a while (an impromptu biscuit offered around the office, a slice of birthday cake). I will eat because my body says it's hungry, because it needs energy to function. I will finally throw away my size zero clothes—I have been putting this off for months now— I'll go through my wardrobe and get rid of anything that might feel tight as I gain weight. (This, by the way, sounds trivial but is incredibly important to recovery.)

I will remember that meals happen three times a day, that *people eat food and use it up and then eat again*: it's OK, it's normal. I won't tell myself that fruit is a meal or that eating a bunch of grapes is OK for lunch. I will gain the 10 or 20 pounds I need and I won't get depressed about this process. I won't panic when people tell me I look "well'; I won't assume they mean "fat."

Of course the fact that I'm setting these rules is part of the problem, isn't it? I need to learn how to relinquish control and instead I'm hanging onto it. But I can only do what I can do. If I redraw the boundaries around food and eating, at least I'll know what I'm aiming for.

And here's the final blow: *I will eat more*. The accepted figure from health experts is 3,500 calories a week to gain or lose a pound of weight. That means I have to eat 500 extra calories a day, in whatever shape or form, and not increase my exercise and not cheat. My sister calls me the food dodger. She says I can spot a bagel coming a mile off and dodge it . . .

So, it's 4 PM and I've eaten a banana today. What's so hard about this? Why, even after this full declaration, can't I just stand up and walk over to the fridge?

Chapter 1

The Fallout

"I've never told anyone this before. I have anorexia.
I'm saying this for the first time in my life."

That was a young man, a complete stranger, writing to me. He was responding to my first article in *The Times*. What he didn't understand was that I was saying it publicly for the first time in my life too.

The column I now write every week had started as a one-off feature—I'd contacted the weekend editor at *The Times* to pitch the idea and she said yes. It was only after the feature was published and readers got in touch saying they wanted to hear more that we realized the potential for a regular column following my journey to beat anorexia.

It was one thing to make the declaration in the newspaper, quite another to follow through. Soon after that first article was published I had a mini-breakdown. I'm no stranger to depression—when you're severely malnourished, it's perfectly logical to feel low—but this was different. I'd decided to tell the world about my deepest secret. I was ashamed, of course, but I was also scared.

By exposing myself in this way, I was acknowledging that something was very wrong in my life. I had declared my hand

and now I'd have to do something about it. "My name is X and I'm an alcoholic" is what they say at AA meetings, right? For my entire adult life I've been pretending I'm fine (*I've already eaten, thanks, I'm not hungry* . . .) but now I was admitting that I wasn't fine at all. And I was doing something I never, ever do: I was asking for help.

What frightens me now is leaving the eating disorder behind. I've been anorexic for more than ten years. It's part of who I am.

* * *

It happened that the weekend my first article appeared in *The Times* we were abroad. Tom was working on his latest book about high-speed travel and how Europe was opening up to the U.K. We'd spent much of that autumn and winter exploring fascinating European cities: Antwerp, Rotterdam, Girona, Bruges, and this weekend, in mid-November, we were in Lausanne. I hadn't told anyone except my family that I was writing a piece about anorexia, and I welcomed the chance to escape.

I will always remember that trip. We arrived at the Beau Rivage Hotel in Lausanne on Friday evening, weary from our early start and the long train journey. As usual on our weekends away, we lit some candles and shared a bubble bath, winding down gradually. We ordered room service and then watched a couple of episodes of *The Wire*. With our incessant traveling we'd become hooked on DVD box sets—from *Downton Abbey* to *Mad Men* to *Shameless*; we always had one on the go. This weekend Tom had bought *The Wire*, a series going back five seasons, which we had both missed the first time around. Even as we watched, episode after convoluted episode, we kept asking each other why *The Wire* had achieved such status as a cult classic. We both agreed the scripts were hopeless, the acting was patchy (Dominic West's American accent was painful!), and the plot lines were incomprehensible—but we too got addicted nonetheless.

We were staying in the penthouse suite, with panoramic views overlooking Lake Geneva. It had an elegant, high-ceilinged bedroom, a separate living room, and a spacious marble bathroom. After dinner we went down to the lake and wandered along the shore in the darkness. It was a chilly evening, but the air was crisp and the sky was full of stars. On our way back we stopped at the hotel bar for a nightcap—Baileys for me, amaretto for Tom—and went to bed around midnight.

I lay awake, worrying about what I'd done. I remember thinking: *The newspaper will be at the printers—It will be in the vans now—What on Earth have I done?—How can I undo this?* I felt as though I had planted a bomb and run away. *Maybe I could stay in Lausanne,* I thought—*Graham Greene spent his final years here after all, it can't be such a bad place*—hiding away from the shameful confession I'd made. Eating disorders are for teenagers, not adults—what would happen next, would I be expected to start eating? I imagined myself starting to eat and never being able to stop. Around 4 AM, I fell into a restless sleep.

Next morning we got up early. Tom was refreshed from a good night's sleep; I was low but kept it to myself. We went downstairs to the swimming pool and spa, a stunning glass creation overlooking the vast blue lagoon. The pool was empty at that time on a Friday morning, although a couple of Swiss bankers pounded the treadmills in the fitness center. We swam a few lengths and gazed out across the lake; I felt revived and restored by the water. Back upstairs, Tom ordered breakfast while I showered, then we sat on the balcony, sipping coffee in our bathrobes.

The newspaper arrived with the breakfast tray. We turned to the *Weekend* section—and there I was, in a pale pink cardigan and dark blue skinny jeans, splashed over a double-page spread. *The Times*'s photographer had been to my flat the previous week, a friendly guy who chatted about a photo shoot with George W. Bush in Texas while he snapped away. I hadn't seen the image they were planning to use, nor the final version of my article. Their headline shocked me: *Diary of an anorexic, aged 32*. My cheeks burned with the shame of the "A" word; was that really me they were talking about? My name stood out in bold: not much room for doubt.

We spread the newspaper on the table between us and read in silence. There it was, anorexia, in black and white for anyone to read. Yes, my aim had been to write an honest article, but I hadn't expected to feel like this. Was I being naive? Confessional journalism was one thing but this was different, like someone getting ahold of my diary and printing it.

I finished reading it and felt . . . OK. A bit raw, but OK. The photograph could have been worse. The headline was awful (that label, "anorexic") but they hadn't messed about with my actual copy. I turned to look at Tom and he had tears rolling down his face. "I'm so proud of you, love." He came around the breakfast table and hugged me.

* * *

Returning to London from that weekend in Lausanne, I was overwhelmed by the response to my original article. I received hundreds of emails—from strangers, friends, old flames. After I got over my initial feelings of shame, I began to see that I wasn't the only one. I already knew that a lot of women felt bad about their bodies. What I didn't realize, until recently, was how bad women felt about their appetites, about being hungry and needing food and the simple act of feeding themselves.

Although anorexia is a predominantly female illness, I began to see how many men are also affected by it. There were emails from husbands, partners, and fathers.

One man wrote:

I have just been discussing your article with my daughter—it's the first time we have ever talked about this. She is eighteen years old and has been anorexic for two years now. She has many of the same thoughts and issues you have expressed, but she seems not to want to change at the moment or accept help.

Another father wrote:

As the father of an anorexic daughter, I read your article with much interest. I also listened to you on Radio 4. Firstly, thank you for being so open and honest about the disease. My daughter has been anorexic for over seven years but is now managing to do a degree at university. I fear that she may never recover or have children, and I wish you and your boyfriend every success. Please keep writing and informing people about how you're coping . . . I am sure it will help others who are battling as you are.

A young male sufferer wrote:

This was painful to read because I know how difficult it is to speak about having an illness like anorexia—I've told only one person since my relationship with food broke down and I lost control of my life. Although our stories are totally different, I felt the words you used were the ones I would if I wasn't still so petrified.

These messages provoked different emotions in me; a weird jumble of positives and negatives. I felt awed that my article had encouraged people to talk about anorexia—a father and daughter broaching the subject for the first time, say—but then I felt panicky that I'd uncovered something I wasn't qualified to follow up on. (It reminded me of being a child and throwing an egg out of a very high window, then looking out to see a furious car-driver below.)

I felt responsible. These were real people's lives: young men who'd never spoken about it, children whose parents were sick with worry. To use the word "anorexia," to admit to problems, is important of course, but it opens a can of worms . . . My intention had been to document my *own* experience, and yet people seemed to relate to it. That was a good lesson for me, early on, in the power of the printed word: I've learned to be careful—still honest, I hope, but careful—about what I write.

A woman emailed:

Your story is so similar yet so different to my own . . . I am thirty-three years old and my ultimate goal is to have a family. My husband has said very similar things [as] your boyfriend. I came out of rehab a year ago this week with the goal of being at a healthy weight and possibly pregnant by the end of this year. Sadly I am actually now in a worse situation and enough is enough.

A younger woman said:

I'm twenty years old and have been battling with eating disorder (ED) thoughts for as long as I can remember. In March of this year I was finally diagnosed with anorexia and I have been in hospital ever since. I am now a day patient and will be discharged from hospital in two weeks' time. Even now, I am far from recovered.

My mind still tortures me for every mouthful I allow myself to eat and I continue to hurt my family and friends by being incapable of letting go of the ED altogether. I feel selfish and weak but am trapped in a vicious circle. I do know, however, that people with EDs are extremely determined and that if we fight we can beat the anorexia. Thank you for your column. I hope people who don't understand the illness will read it. Good luck. Don't give in. You will have the family you want and deserve.

Reading those messages I was reminded of how fortunate I'd been, avoiding hospitals and rehabilitation clinics. Anorexia can get a lot more severe than mine. (Am I a fraud?)

A middle-aged woman emailed:

I read your article and cried. I'm a forty-three-year-old mother of two beautiful girls aged eight and six. Daily I hate myself for being so selfish as to "put anorexia" before everything else but as you know, it is a vicious, horrible disease. I would never have chosen to be ill with anorexia in a million years. However I am now on the very slow path to recovery.

Another woman wrote:

This is like reading my life on a page. The Oxford exams struggled through, the social meals lost, the addiction to starvation persevering all the while . . . you're right that every day spent this way is a waste. One day I am scared I will look back and realize that my one and only chance at life has slipped through my fingers. By then it will be too late. I am a stuck record, in the grip of a voice that has become so familiar, I no longer know where it ends and mine begins. Or even if they are different at all. I have got to do the same things as you; your challenge is mine. Impromptu eating, not jumping out of bed onto the treadmill, following rules that will help rather than hurt me now. It feels both slightly odd and a comfort to recognize doppelgänger thoughts in another woman. Eating is what it takes, but it's harder than all the other therapies put together. In itself it's the medicine. I'll eat if you can.

That really got me: *I'll eat if you can.*

A middle-aged female general practitioner wrote:

I wish you all the best. I am impressed you are sticking to this so admirably and I'm trying to be as strong as you are. Your column is taped to my freezer and helps me force open the door, actually remove food, and even eat it! Keep going, we are stronger than this and surely must have so much to gain. I am keeping my fingers crossed for you—and all of us trying.

That amazed me: to think of a GP, a professional working woman, with my column taped to the door of her freezer! One assumes that "grown-ups" with real careers don't get eating disorders, but it's not true.

A psychologist wrote to say:

Your article communicates powerfully the impact of an eating disorder. I wish you all the luck in the world, but if this attempt doesn't work please don't beat yourself up. I do have concerns about this sort of "reality" journalism in terms of the pressure it places on the individual in the public gaze, especially as you've used your true identity. I will follow your online column with great interest.

A lot of support and encouragement, but that psychologist was right—also a lot of pressure.

* * *

After the weekend in Lausanne when it all felt unreal, after the initial euphoria faded, after interviews on Radio 4's *Woman's Hour* and the BBC World Service, after meetings with publishers —that was when I collapsed. I describe it as a mini-breakdown because that's how it felt. I started crying for the first time in years and couldn't stop. I stayed in my flat for seven days straight. I felt too raw to go outside. I didn't answer the phone or check my emails. I stopped eating—a violent reaction to the decision to give up anorexia—and I stopped sleeping. I took hot baths and read T. S. Eliot (always good in a crisis) and drifted around in tracksuit bottoms—and cried.

It's an amazing thing, to feel the ability to cry returning. That week was bad, but I think those tears were the first step on the road to recovery. With anorexia, you're so frozen and isolated; it's like some kind of locked-in syndrome. You still experience human emotions—regret, envy, despair—but it's all pretty insular, sort of muted. Your body goes into emergency mode: focusing on essentials only, conserving energy, keeping you alive. Just as your periods stop because you can't nurture a baby— your body can't risk getting pregnant—any excess emotions dry up. With so little fuel going in, there's simply nothing to spare.

Growing up, I'd always been extreme—a natural Scorpio. I was "in touch" with my emotions: love and hate, excitement, drama and disaster. As anorexia set in, all that dried up. Those natural ups and downs, female hormones, the premenstrual moods and tears seemed to disappear completely. So when I started crying I was fearful, yes, but it was also a huge release. Finally, I was being honest about this illness I'd been denying for years. Now I was going to have to do something about it.

All those people who wrote to thank me—I should thank them. Despite my mixed emotions, their responses made my selfish desire to get a life seem less selfish. It depersonalized my struggle and gave me a mission. At the heart of anorexia is a belief that you're not really worth a damn. You don't deserve to listen to your body or respond to your hunger: basically, you don't deserve to eat. With all these people reading my story, following my journey and gunning for me, I had a reason to commit to recovery.

Of course, I want to show other sufferers it is possible to get better. The line that really stood out, that I still repeat to myself, was this: *I'll eat if you can.* That's why people email me every week, because anorexia is lonely and frightening, because you need reassurance every step of the way. *I'll eat if you can.* That's the promise I made to all those strangers; that's the promise they're making to me.

* * *

As well as for them, I did it for myself, because I was desperate for a solution. Anorexia is an addiction and a compulsion, a brain disorder and a crutch. When I use the word "addiction," I don't use it lightly. In my case, I am addicted to hunger.

I set myself the challenge in public because I didn't know what else to do: I hoped it would succeed where everything else— therapy, drugs, and determination—had failed. The question I had been avoiding for ten years wouldn't go away: how long was I planning to starve myself? I've always prided myself on honesty, clarity of thought and expression, but anorexia involves a remarkable amount of self-deceit. As much as I denied the problem, to others and to myself, I couldn't keep looking the other way. Something had shaken me up: the thought of having a baby maybe, finding myself in my early thirties, or just a longing to take part in life again. I knew that with anorexia I'd stay trapped forever.

And then there was Tom. Even if I didn't believe I could recover from anorexia—even if I didn't want to save myself—I had to think about him now too.

Chapter 2
Love at First Sight?

When Tom and I met I wasn't looking for a man and I certainly wasn't looking for love. To be honest, I wasn't even in the mood to go out—it was a drizzly February evening and I'd been at the office since 7 AM. At that time I was Commissioning Editor at a London publisher (I've been in publishing since the age of twenty-one, mostly in psychology and the humanities). Work had been the usual round of exasperating meetings, and I wasn't in the mood to be chatty or sociable. All I really wanted was to cycle home, take a long hot bath, and spend a few hours reading before bed. I have no idea what had impelled me to agree to the blind date in the first place; I didn't have time for myself, let alone a new boyfriend.

A mixture of curiosity and politeness overcame my reluctance— it would be rude to cancel on this guy at the last minute, and I was a little bit intrigued. Also, why on Earth had I been set up? The matchmaker responsible was my mother's best friend's daughter Leo; I hadn't seen her for years—hardly a close confidante. I wondered what it was about him and me that had made Leo think the two of us should meet.

I decided to go along, but just for one drink. If he's an oddball or boring, I'll simply make conversation for half an hour and then excuse myself, I thought as I changed in the ladies' room at work.

My midnight blue silk top with dark blue jeans (smart but also sexy, in case the date went well), a spritz of perfume and some fresh makeup, and I was ready to go.

That night, weaving my way through Hammersmith Broadway in the rain, I wasn't exactly nervous, just slightly uneasy. I didn't know what to expect. To be honest, I assumed that any guy who suggested meeting for a blind date in Hammersmith would be a loser. I had no idea meeting Tom would change everything.

I pushed open the glass doors of the Lyric Bar and paused for a moment. Three or four men glanced up but I had no idea which one I was looking for. It was probably no more than a minute that I stood there, but it felt like ages. Then a bespectacled young man rushed up, waving a book, and I knew this must be Tom. He was small and neatly dressed, and looked somehow familiar. Kermit the Frog, or Casper the Friendly Ghost? No, the broadcaster Andrew Marr, that was it, the glasses and the ears, a kind of geeky seriousness. He wore a pale blue shirt under a navy cashmere sweater, and a pair of blue jeans. Good leather shoes, I noticed.

Our first exchange was the usual flurry of introductions and apologies: *Are you . . . You must be . . . I hope I didn't keep you waiting . . .* and then an awkward moment, standing at the bar while he bought me a glass of wine. Then we sat down at a table in the corner; the lights were low and there was classical music playing quietly. Tom was halfway down a bottle of Peroni, I saw, so he must have been here a while, or maybe he was just nervous.

After a few sips of our drinks we both began to relax and warm up. The first topic of conversation was, of course, this blind date— we both confessed to having deep misgivings about it in advance, and it turned out we had both wanted to cancel. This broke the ice, and from that point on there were no silences. At one point, waiting at the bar to buy another round of drinks, I remember smiling to myself and thinking, *So, that's Tom. It could be worse.*

It was hardly a *coup de foudre*; I didn't want to rip his clothes off or elope with him, but I was enjoying the evening. I'd abandoned my plan to climb out through the window of the ladies' restroom.

That first date ended in the not-so-romantic surroundings of the Hammersmith tube station. The fluorescent strip lighting was an unwelcome contrast to the mellow atmosphere of the Lyric Bar and the mood was somewhat broken. People jostled past us by the entrance to the Piccadilly line and we were awkward again as we said goodbye. Tom scrabbled to find a business card and couldn't, so I gave him one of mine. I sat on the last train home, wondering what I thought of him, whether I wanted to see him again. I was unsure.

My mum, my best friend, my sisters texted and called: *So, how did it go? What's this Tom guy like? Do you think he's the one?* I didn't know what to answer. *We talked a lot*, I remember telling them. Turns out we haven't stopped talking since.

* * *

I don't know when I fell in love with Tom; maybe it happened gradually, over those first few months. We spent more and more time together, and traveled a lot, and slowly our lives began to merge. We made plans that stretched further into the future, in that tentative way of early relationships. We discussed ideas and read each other's writing, we shared books and music, we met each other's families. Both quite cerebral people, we began to open up. But I never intended to share my "problems," especially not when it came to food. If I'm honest, I still massively resent the intrusion into my personal issues. Except of course it's not just *my* problem.

This is something it has taken me a long time to accept—this eating disorder isn't just about me. As a fiercely private person, I felt (and still feel) that I shouldn't have to account for anorexia, that it's my choice to eat or not eat. I'm the one who's hungry all the time—why is that anyone else's business? My father's motto for life, "Never apologize, never explain," has always been a personal mantra of mine, but this time it won't wash. I can't keep pretending everything's normal when it's not. My hang-ups about food affect things outside of me, especially my relationships.

* * *

Left to my own devices, I would never have discussed anorexia with him. It sort of surfaced naturally a few months after we'd met. Tom is a travel journalist for a national newspaper and we were on a trip, as usual. (That first year together, we spent forty-seven out of fifty-two weekends away from London.) This time we were in Copenhagen to review an exclusive new eco-hotel and spa.

A luxury hotel and spa treatments and a beautiful city to explore? It should have been perfect. But somehow it was one of those weekends that started out wrong and got worse. Maybe it was exhaustion, or lack of food, or my own depressive nature, but I spent the whole time struggling to get back on track. Waiting at Heathrow Airport, I remember standing at the sink in the restroom close to tears. I wondered how I could get through the next five minutes, let alone the weekend. That was unlike me—sure, I go up and down, but I don't do weepy.

The flight out of London was delayed due to fog over the Channel; we arrived in Copenhagen late on Friday evening in a rainstorm. After eating a quick supper we'd picked up (a hot dog for Tom, a banana for me) we unpacked a few things and fell into bed. Tom reached out to touch me, to hold me—he'd been on assignment in Colombia for ten days—to cuddle me goodnight.

But my body was tense and I curled away from him, unable to respond. I didn't want to kiss him, I didn't want to be touched.

We lay there in the dark, me almost falling off the edge of the bed, clutching at the duvet, Tom reaching all the way over. After a few minutes of silence he sighed and said my name out loud into the silent bedroom. I said nothing, waiting, wishing he would go to sleep. He reached up and stroked the back of my neck, teasing at tendrils of hair, and I felt nothing. It was so quiet I could hear us both blinking. I wanted to scream; I wanted to leave.

Finally Tom said, "Emma, please. What's the matter?" I said nothing. "I've been missing you, longing for you, love. I've been away from you for nearly two weeks and all I want to do is hold you in my arms." This was strong stuff from Tom—in those early days, he wasn't versed in the art of romantic-speak, although he's pretty good now. Still I didn't know what to say. It wasn't about sex, just that I didn't feel close to anyone or anything; I didn't want to be held. I felt I would snap.

We lay there for ages, in silence. Eventually, I reached across and kissed his forehead. I found his hand and we lay in the large four-poster bed, holding hands. After ten minutes or so Tom's steady breathing told me he was asleep. I lay awake, unable to get control of my racing mind. It seems impossible to me that one can be so tired and still not sleep, but I've never learned how to switch off. The hours that followed in Copenhagen were some of the lowest I remember. Strange how you can be lying next to another person and feel so completely alone. I went from exhaustion to anger—looking at Tom's sleeping face, calm and peaceful—to despair. Around 5 AM I stood up, wound one of the white sheets around me and opened the door to the fire escape. It was cold and still raining. I sat down on the metal stairwell outside.

Before long, Tom appeared in the doorway, fuddled with sleep. He tried to coax me inside, into the warmth, to come back to bed, but I couldn't move from the chilly metal stairs. I held my head in my hands and he held me. I was dizzy from lack of sleep (not just that night but the many weeks and months before) and unable to speak. Everything seemed hopeless; everything seemed as bleak as the gray morning light. Somewhere Tom's gentle voice went on, explaining how we could change things, how he would help; he rubbed my hands to warm me but I couldn't feel anything. We sat that way for ages, shivering, wrapped in a few thin sheets, his head resting on my shoulder. My clearest memory is thinking, *Poor Tom, this is not the romantic mini-break he signed up for.*

It was there on the stairwell as dawn broke and rain fell that we finally talked openly about anorexia.

* * *

Tom had been reading about insomnia on the Internet, trying to understand what was going on, and he had some theories about the cause. In my case, my diet. He explained, "Em, you're doing huge amounts of exercise and sometimes you don't eat all day. I'm no expert, but think about it, by the time you lie down at the end of the day your body is simply in deficit; it can't unwind because it's not relaxed. You need to eat more throughout the day; it's just about meeting your energy requirements. If you ate regularly, your body would be able to relax at night and switch off. Don't you think?" He was closer than he realized, of course, and I nodded, awkward and silent. Of course it seems obvious now, but this was the first time we'd discussed it; I felt unmasked, as if he'd been reading my thoughts.

I explained to Tom, as if I were being rational, that I had lost the ability to sleep. And I couldn't stand up or go back to bed, I couldn't go downstairs to the breakfast room, because I simply couldn't go on . . . After listening to this monotone patiently he finally took control, marched into the bathroom, and ran me a bubble bath.

It's miraculous the way something as simple as a cup of coffee or a hot bath can rescue us at a moment of real crisis. Otherwise how would we go on? I think this is what separates humans from animals.

I lay back in the bath and Tom closed the door. I could hear him through the wall, straightening up the bedroom. (I would feel guilty except that I have tidied so many hotel rooms after him—wet towels on bathroom floors and bedrooms littered with wine glasses.) I was ashamed of myself, uneasy with the night's events. I wasn't used to showing anyone my weakness. I soaked the washcloth in the hot scented water and brought it to my face, pressed down on my cheeks and forehead, massaged my aching eye sockets. It was dark and warm beneath the damp compress. I wanted to stay in that bath, eyes closed, hiding from it all. It was just a hot bath, but it saved me.

When I was wrapped in a white bathrobe and sitting on the newly made bed, Tom went downstairs for a breakfast tray, carefully selecting foods he knew I could eat. In a parallel universe—the world without anorexia—I would start the day with Danish pastries or croissants, buttered toast and raspberry jam, nutty bread or sourdough or oven-warm rolls. Yes, I love food—I love the same delicious food as everyone else. But I can't eat it.

Instead I had gallons of coffee and a plate of fruit: chunks of pineapple, sliced kiwi, and strawberries. I realized how good it tasted and how dehydrated I was from lack of food and sleep. Tom checked that I had enough coffee and then ate quickly: two slices of toast and a brown roll with cheese and ham.

How come he could eat? This is one of those stupid petulant thoughts you have with an eating disorder: *Why is he so greedy? How does he eat all that lovely food and stay slim while I have to starve myself?* You crunch grimly through another apple, not thinking clearly about the fact that no one is stopping you from eating; in fact they would do anything to feed you those healthy foods too.

After breakfast we sat on the bed in our bathrobes talking, our heads resting together against the pillows. Tom reminded me of the positives, all the good stuff in life, everything we have to look forward to. For the first time he talked about children. "Remember how much you love babies; just think of how wonderful it will be when you have one of your own." I realized we were talking about having babies together, and my heart banged hard against my chest. Tom continued, "At the airport yesterday, remember that family and their children—when I watched you playing with that tiny baby, I'd never seen anything so beautiful, Em. And I've seen you with Katie's children"—my big sister Katie has three children, two girls and a newborn boy. "I've seen you holding baby Theo and I know you'll be such a natural mother."

I didn't want to ruin that moment, for it was special, but I knew I had to tell him the truth. I managed to murmur something that I knew Tom needed to know, something to the effect that I can't necessarily have babies at the moment. I can't recall what I said but it was incomplete and ashamed, for that's how I felt and still feel. Tom asked me a few questions, quietly, gently. He said he would support me to eat more, a little at a time. This frightened me of course; any thought of eating more still threatens my stubborn sense of autonomy. He told me that I'd never get fat, just that I needed to eat for my fertility, my sleep, our happiness.

It was important to talk about it, I know that now, but God, I felt exposed. I knew I couldn't go on with this secret forever; that's what adults do: they talk about difficult things. Tom didn't judge me or scorn; in fact he didn't seem that surprised. He had already made the link between how little I eat and how much I exercise; he understood my vague references to ovaries "shutting down." I explained it was temporary and reversible: according to my doctors I'm not infertile, just underweight. Tom kept saying he loved me and would do anything to help me get better, a little at a time.

Once the eating disorder topic was out there it amazed me that we were discussing it. The language was slightly evasive, but we were actually talking about it. We talked of low body fat, my overly healthy lifestyle (*ha!*), excessive exercise, but we did not use the term "anorexia." In fact we never said "anorexia" until *The Times* printed it—and to this day we both still hesitate before using that word.

* * *

For the rest of the weekend it was as though a layer of skin had been peeled away from me: I was raw. What I remember now from Copenhagen—as well as the eco-hotel and the sauna and cycling in the rain around the hippie suburb of Christiania—was that time with Tom, that new beginning. Ever since that terrible night and morning, there's been a new level of openness between us. How amazing: this man, who accepts me as I am.

But it isn't stable; nothing is. Sometimes I'm glad he understands and loves me anyway; at other times I feel angry at the invasion of my privacy. When I'm having an episode of the "mean reds" I think Tom needs me to be weak like this, broken. Most men like to feel useful: does my being "unwell" give him a useful purpose? Maybe this "saving me from myself" enables him to reach me in a way that my cast-iron barriers don't normally allow?

A few days after we got back from Copenhagen I was talking to my big sister, trying to explain how exposed I felt. Thinking back to that conversation with Katie I can see how frightened I was. It wasn't anger with Tom so much as fear of recovery, the same old fear of opening up: that someone would help me, would force me to face this.

Was it the right thing to have done? Share and share until he knows everything, until there's nothing left for me? Ever since we talked about food and weight and health issues, it seems I'm expected to be open about everything. I have always found this difficult: at times I feel prickly, uncomfortable in my own skin. It nags at me that he knows so much; now that we've discussed anorexia, there's nothing private left. Why must I tell him everything just because we're in a relationship? Sometimes I feel stripped of my dignity; I want to run very far away.

Even now, two years later, I still feel a sense of loss. Why did we talk—why did I open up like that in Copenhagen? I've been forced into sharing and I hate it: this is my problem, my private hell, this is for real. Now my issues about eating are casual conversation topics: *We need to fatten you up*; *I'm going to bring you a bagel*; *Promise me you won't skip lunch*. I never wanted anyone to help me, I never asked for it.

* * *

Tom and I have been through turmoil, but there's also a lot of happiness. We talk and laugh and read and write endlessly, we're always running off for another adventure, or calling each other with new schemes and plans, lying in bed together, or sharing a bath.

Would I have done this on my own? I'm not sure. In many ways this relationship with Tom is central to my journey of recovery. Despite our individual failings—my stubborn independence, his irrational jealousy (of any man who comes within a mile radius of me—any male friend, colleague, acquaintance, or stranger)—

mostly it seems to work. On that rainy February evening, that unlikely blind date, we found each other—and we might even make it through. No relationship is perfect, and I think we're both learning to compromise.

* * *

One morning last week, for example, a burst of optimism. Usually I find January the bleakest month but this year I feel positive, full of hope: it's a new year and I'm determined to make progress. I had stayed overnight at Tom's flat, and we were sitting at the breakfast table, sharing the newspaper, discussing the headlines, grumbling companionably about going to work, sipping our coffee and eating—raspberries for me, toast and jam for Tom. I'd slept badly and the tiredness would catch up with me later, but for the time being there was nowhere else I'd have rather been. I looked at Tom, his hair wet from the shower, his blue shirt and jeans, gobbling his toast as if it would run away, and I felt acutely happy. After so many years of guarding my own space, it feels good to be normal: sitting at the breakfast table, eating together, starting the day with another human being.

I cycled off to work. Two hours later I received this email: *Em, I believe in you absolutely. I'm filled with hope about the future for us and hope you are too ... Waking up next to you in the morning is the best way to start the day. When I think of my life a few years ago when you didn't exist for me, it was just a different existence, as though I was living on another planet. T x*

There is so much worth struggling for; when our relationship is good it's the best. Tom and I have been through a lot, but he can stay or go; he is an adult and it's his choice. I recall that line in *On the Road*, "I had nothing to offer anybody except my own confusion," and wonder why he's with me ... but I'm starting to understand that most of us feel this way most of the time, a bit ramshackle, a bit confused.

If there's any point to love, surely it's to make us strive to be better people—kinder, more generous. With Tom, I want to be a nicer version of me for him. Every day I try to think of myself less, to put him first, to get outside the depression and anxiety of the eating disorder. As anyone who has been close to a sufferer will know, anorexia is more than a problem with food. It doesn't just surface at mealtimes. It's a constant conflict, a state of internal warfare. Yes, it's like I've declared war on myself.

I often remember something my great-aunt, Virginia Woolf, wrote in her novel *Night and Day*: "Of course I behave badly, but you can't judge people by what they do. You can't go through life measuring right and wrong with a foot rule." Don't get me wrong: it's no excuse. I'm responsible for everything I do and say. I try not to blame my bad behavior on anorexia, but remember this is not a diet gone wrong; it's a mental illness.

Mental illness, sickness, disease—I never thought I'd be involved in any of this. I don't enjoy appointments with doctors or psychiatrists, and I don't think of myself as a victim. But who knows what life has in store for you—and who knows who you'll fall in love with? I know this has been a huge learning curve for Tom, but I am who I am, and this condition is what it is. Would it sound lame if I said that anorexia was never my choice?

I do have a choice now, and that's to recover. So, I keep trying.

Chapter 3
It's a Family Affair

There was another reason I decided to out myself: it was also for my family. So much worse than going through this myself has been watching what I've put other people through: the constant anxiety etched on their faces; my inability to eat, their inability to pull me out of this trap. Worst of all has been watching what anorexia does to the family, especially to my parents. My mum and dad dreaded every new twist into this anorexic descent, never knowing what to expect next, how much more food I could cut out.

For an illness that is so focused on individual self-destruction, anorexia has surprisingly long tentacles. I thought it was "my own business" but it soon spread all around me, snaking its way into the heart of my family. And while I was busy with the painful private struggle, it wasn't just me who was suffering.

I remember one evening in those early years when I was at my thinnest, twenty years old, in my bedroom at home. I couldn't sleep because I hadn't eaten all day: the cramps and the acid were eating away at my stomach lining; my bones ached on the mattress, unable to settle in a comfortable position. Finally I got out of bed and crept downstairs to make a hot drink—peppermint or camomile, anything calorie-free to ease the hunger. There was a light on in the kitchen so I stopped in the hallway, realizing that my parents were still up, not wanting to interrupt. As I turned to go back upstairs, I overheard my mum saying to my dad, " . . . but I just feel so helpless, watching her starve."

How could I hear something like that and carry on not eating? I know how selfish it was (and still is), how self-centered it all sounds. I could pretend I was just in denial, but it's not as simple as that. I was aware of the pain I was causing my parents, but I had shut myself off. Even if I'd wanted to stop, I didn't know how to. Back then, the anorexia was stronger than everything else.

That Christmas, I had arrived back from university for the holidays in a desperate state, both physically and mentally. The journey, less than two hours from Oxford, had been a struggle: it was a bitterly cold December day and I shivered in my long winter coat. I walked from the bus stop to my parents' house in Camden, hunched like an old lady against the wind. I was dropping below 85 pounds at this point and I knew I was in trouble. I remember wondering whether I could hide the weight loss from my family, and how I'd avoid eating for the next couple of weeks.

I hadn't seen my little sister Alice for months—she'd been living in Rome with her boyfriend, Simone. She's barely two years younger than I am; we're very close and I was looking forward to seeing her. Al threw open the front door, all winter suntan and stylish Italian jeans, came forward to hug me, and burst into tears. The last time she'd seen me I'd been slim, and now here was this skeleton. She'd spoken to my mum while she'd been in Italy of course, she knew they were worried about my weight, but seeing it for herself was another matter. Now, in February of my year of this recovery challenge, I ask Al what she remembers of that night so many years ago. She replies, "You looked like a little sparrow, Em, totally fragile—like you'd snap in two. I hugged you and you were so thin I felt terrified." Weight loss can happen very quickly once anorexia gets a grip. That winter, I was in free fall.

Was I aware, really, or is this just hindsight? At the time I thought I was hiding it well: I'd wear multiple layers of clothing, partly to hide my frame and partly to conserve my dwindling body heat. I wore leggings under my jeans, then vests and tops and sweaters and a hoodie. I wore scarves all the time. But of course I wasn't kidding anyone—the more layers you wear the more baggy and hollow you look. I simply couldn't get warm. I remember spending the entire Christmas holiday either curled up next to the radiator in the living room (burning my back), shivering in scaldingly hot baths, or lying in my bedroom under two duvets.

The guilt is immense and there are so many sad memories. Even though I was living independently by this point, away at university, then in my own flat in London, still the illness polluted my family. Almost every memory from my early twenties is colored with my parents' anxiety—and my own awareness of what I was putting them through. The fear in their eyes, the way they watched me constantly, pleaded with me. What could they do? They tried everything. They learned very quickly that there was no point in forcing me to eat, they knew they mustn't nag, they knew they had to keep encouraging me gently, reassuring me; meanwhile they had to watch their child getting thinner and refusing to eat. It's an awful thing to do to the people you love.

I think it's been particularly hard for my father. Dad was born in 1927 and he's an old-school gentleman: he leaps to his feet whenever a woman enters the room; he never wears brown shoes after 6 PM; he can't understand why people walk around with their shirts "hanging out." Even though he's the fittest, strongest eightysomething I know, and still runs his own publishing company, cycles all over London, and will take on any roofing, rewiring, or plumbing job my mother needs doing, still my father is from a different era. At the age of sixteen, he ran away from his aristocratic home in Buckinghamshire, abandoning a place at Oxford University, and signed up as a trooper. He became a captain in the Royal Armoured Corps, seeing active service in Egypt and the British Mandate of Palestine. As children we always used to ask Dad to tell us about the war: when he talked about "leading his men" our hearts swelled with pride. As well as the Second World War, Dad has been through a lot: the suicide of both parents and his own stormy first marriage to an older Italian actress.

Then one day in his forties he walked into the Reading Room of the British Library, saw a beautiful young woman wearing a miniskirt—my mother—and Cleopatra eyeliner, her dark hair in a beehive. He held open the door for her, invited her for a coffee, and they fell in love. The course of true love wasn't exactly smooth, but they eventually married and had five children.

In other words, my dad has lived a lot. But for all his experience, I think anorexia is still a genuine mystery to him (and to many men). Back when Dad was a young man, the concepts of size zero and body dysmorphia simply didn't exist. In those days young women idolized Marilyn Monroe; they wanted curves and bosoms, not washboard stomachs and boyish hips. In the 1940s and 50s it was the hourglass shape that was sexy, not this modern, androgynous, straight-up-and-down figure. Dad is of that generation born between the two world wars in Britain, a time of rationing and hardship, loss and sacrifice and real hunger: Why would anyone willingly restrict a healthy intake of food?

My mother and I often joke that I'll never find anyone to marry because she's already found him. And that's the truth: not that I want to marry my father, but that I've spent my whole life looking for someone as kind, generous, and loving as he is. He would do anything for any of us, especially his girls, but in the face of anorexia he was powerless. To see me struggling with this invisible mental illness (and the all-too-visible results) tortured him.

I remember that Dad would buy me "treats"—as if I could be tempted to eat, as if delicious food could somehow overcome the irrationality of the eating disorder. I couldn't be "tempted"—it's just something that anorexia doesn't permit. Even after a long day working, even on the harshest winter evenings, he would put on his navy blue cashmere greatcoat and walk up to Camden High Street. It still breaks my heart to think of him coming back from Marks & Spencer with those bagfuls of treats. He would come into the house, bringing a rush of cold air from the dark wintry streets, and smile, call me "Emsie." I'd be sitting at our large wooden table in the kitchen—the table on which Leonard and Virginia Woolf started the Hogarth Press, the table on which they printed T.S. Eliot's *The Waste Land*, and on which we've eaten every family meal for the last thirty years. Dad would find me drinking black coffee, huddled near the radiator, trying to concentrate on translating Chaucer to drive away the hunger pangs, and he'd unpack the green bags from Marks & Spencer: French cheeses—brie and camembert—wonderful salads, warm bread, fresh pasta, delicate pastries—anything to encourage me to eat. It smelled so wonderful and I was starving hungry and I would sit there, terrified.

* * *

But this terror doesn't stem from family hang-ups with food, I don't think. Yesterday, for example, another birthday (February and March are full of birthdays in our family), which means lots of birthday meals at my parents' house. I watch my brothers eating, or my father, and it's quite different from the way my female friends eat. On the whole, men seem to relish their meals. Watching them, I'm reminded of the point of food: it's fuel for our bodies and mind—it's a pleasurable sensation; it's delicious.

Often they hunch over their plates and really set about it: the whole messy, sloppy business of feeding time. Sure, they look like cavemen sometimes: licking their fingers, scooping up sauce with bread, eating in short, concentrated bursts, piling it in. Unlike most of the women I know, they don't pretend they're "not that hungry," or toy with their food. They don't pause and lay down their knives and forks at regular intervals; they don't talk much while they're concentrating on stuffing their faces. I've noticed a lot of women, on the other hand, order delicate meals that don't amount to much—a few bites of steamed fish and a plain side salad—and then string out these meals with endless conversation. No wonder these lunches require large glasses of white wine. Obviously I don't do this kind of social lunching myself (friends have long since given up asking me to meet for lunch), but it doesn't look very hearty. I walk past cafés and restaurants where women are sitting together, chatting over plates of salads, and I wonder, *Is that all they're having?* I feel greedy for thinking this—but don't they get hungry and want to stop off for a sandwich on the way home?

In general, most men don't take much notice of what other men are having—they eat and then they stop. They order what they feel like eating, not what their friends order. In general, women are much more conscious of what their friends are ordering— and more importantly what they eat and what they leave on the plate (or tucked under a salad leaf). If men order fries they'll eat them—but not if they're not hungry. I've often seen Tom order a hamburger, and it'll come with a pile of French fries. This doesn't bother him in the slightest; if he's full from the hamburger, he just leaves the fries. He doesn't keep looking at them and fiddling with them and sneaking in one fry and then another. He either eats them or he doesn't, but it's no big deal.

My brothers and my father have also taught me a lot about how to eat. Enjoy your food and stop when you're full. Don't fuss about. Surely this is the answer to obesity and anorexia and emotional eating—a natural relationship with food, a responsive attitude to one's own appetite?

If only the solution to anorexia were that simple. I can only explain it like this—the less you eat, the more scared you are of eating; the longer you starve, the more addicted you become to hunger, that clean, empty high.

What does anorexia give me, what is this high? It fills me with endorphins, adrenaline; it gives me a pure, healthy feeling, a buzz, a sense of achievement, a sense of control. The hunger is the drug. Forget cocaine, forget Ecstasy, this is the best high I've ever known. Logically, hunger should make you weak and listless, right? Not so with anorexia: the mania has always driven me to run faster, cycle farther, stay up later, read more, eat less. The longer you do it, the more you realize that anorexics are superhuman: I don't know what I've been running on all these years, but it doesn't seem to run out.

A reader wrote to tell me he had once tried to eat the same food (fruit and vegetables) as his anorexic girlfriend for a week, just to see what it was like. I don't know what the point of it was: to prove to her that she wasn't eating enough, to understand her eating habits for himself? By the first evening he was dizzy and in a foul mood—after a day of just grapes and carrots he seriously thought he'd faint on the tube home from work. The experiment was abandoned, he wrote, much to the relief of them both.

And yet it surprises me that everyone doesn't have anorexia. It's safe and measurable: it delivers. In such an unpredictable world, it seems like a logical way to live. My approach to eating— regimented, organized, every bite accounted for—doesn't seem "disordered" or abnormal. It would frighten me to eat as others do—that impulsive, unnoticed chocolate biscuit; the unscheduled slice of birthday cake in the office, the quick sandwich eaten on the hoof while waiting for the bus.

How can you eat like that? All those hidden extras—the lack of planning in food—I find it unsettling, erratic. Weight-loss experts have long known this: how easily people forget what they've eaten, how they underestimate their actual daily food intake. At the heart of my problem is this need to stay in control—and of course the ever-present fear of letting go. Honestly, I think everyone else is out of control. I can't relax around food; to me it's a risk, a flashing red light, a time to be vigilant.

I see people eating potato chips while walking down the street, or grazing on peanuts in a wine bar, and I just don't get it.

* * *

Part of this journey of recovery, and part of growing up, is that I have to accept I'm wrong. Simple as that. However much I believe that my (restrictive) approach to food is correct and that everyone else is excessive and out of control, I have to accept that the world sees it differently. Whatever I think is right—is wrong. This is unsustainable. Anorexia ruins relationships and wrecks your health. It traps you in a prison of your own making and isolates you from your family. I've done enough damage. I'll always carry the isolation inside me.

From the age of nineteen, as anorexia took hold, I avoided physical contact with my parents—it was simply too much to bear, too close. Back in the Oxford years, hovering in the kitchen around mealtimes, wanting the warmth of human company after months of self-imposed solitude at university, transfixed by the smell and look of food I couldn't eat, as well as by the heat from the oven, I'd talk to Mum and sometimes she'd reach out her arms. I wanted so much to admit that I was tired of fighting myself, to let her look after me, but the fear and vigilance kept me stiff and unhuggable. I needed to stay strong. I feared that if

I asked for help or let my guard down, even for a moment, I'd collapse completely. My fear of being weak and needy was linked to the fear of becoming fat and greedy (it still is). So this created a physical and emotional distance between me and the others, a distance I was unaccustomed to. As children, we'd fight to sit at Dad's feet for the bedtime story—he would read *A Christmas Carol* to the five of us, every December, the highlight of our year. I often cuddled my mum, occasionally even my brothers or sisters . . . but anorexia had made me so wary.

Even now when my mum and dad hug me, a little part of me still wonders if they're checking—checking for the bony spine, the jutting shoulder blades—the way they used to when I was hiding under all those layers of clothes.

* * *

Whenever I think about my family and anorexia, I think about birthdays. We make a big deal of birthdays in my family—not only us five kids and Mum and Dad, but now the husband and children of my big sister (Charlie, Virginia, Isla, and Theo) and the wife and children of my big brother (Katrina, Leonard, and Julian). So there are frequent gatherings at my parents' house and, inevitably, lots of food occasions.

As well as birthdays, there's the annual Christmas extravaganza (which admittedly gets more fun as the little ones arrive). Sometimes I look around the kitchen table at my family, these people I love, handing out plates, helping each other to sticky toffee pudding or cheesecake, brandy-filled trifle or fruitcake, sharing forkfuls of meringue, squabbling over the last flapjack.

It's when we're all together that I feel most trapped by my illness. I want to join in, I want to share the fun and eat with them, but it's been so long. I've forgotten how. Gripping my mug of black coffee more tightly, I feel distinctly not part of the family. (If they offer me a slice of cake I feel awkward, and if they don't bother to offer me any I feel angry.) I want to be a part of all that rowdy, pleasurable eating, but I can't.

This is when I feel like the death's head at the feast. It is hard to describe, this paralysis when faced with food in company: a low-fat slice of lemon drizzle cake, a small biscuit; anything, basically.

* * *

A few months ago, back in December, it was my sister Katie's birthday. Tom and I had been away for the weekend, reviewing hotels in Cornwall. He dropped me off at my flat around 3 PM and I showered, changed, and cycled over to Camden for 4 PM. We gathered in the living room over cups of tea, and Mum had made the most amazing cake: three layers of fluffy, buttery sponge, held together with fresh cream and raspberries, and slatherings of milk chocolate on top, dripping down the sides. It looked unbearably delicious: my mouth actually watered with yearning . . .

But of course I couldn't. We sang "Happy Birthday" to Katie and she blew out the candles and Mum doled out big slices of cake, while I just sat there feeling wretched. (And hungrier than usual, since it had been a difficult day food-wise and I couldn't face lunch.) Everyone had second helpings—even my two sisters and my mum, all of whom are slim.

Have you ever tried to encourage someone with an eating disorder to eat a small slice of chocolate cake, just to celebrate their own birthday, say? It's not stubbornness: they literally cannot do it. Can you imagine not being able to relax enough to take part in your own birthday party? A tiny bite of cake? I can't do it.

Cake aside, you can probably see that my family matters a lot to me. And that's a massive part of the motivation to beat anorexia.

I'm sick of putting them through this, sick of seeing their worried glances when I dare to wear a T-shirt . . . Because I know it's still not right, the way I look. At Katie's birthday, for example, I'd worn a new Oasis top that Tom had bought me in Cornwall— just a simple tee, sky blue, short capped sleeves. Alice and Mum exchanged a glance at one point, a glance I know too well, and I got a glimpse of myself in the large antique mirror opposite. As I laughed and gesticulated with my family, my hands looked like huge flapping things on the end of scarecrow-thin arms.

I want to start my own family, and I want to make it up to the family I already have. Anorexia has haunted their lives for too long.

Chapter 4

The Personal is Political

So, if "coming out" about my eating disorder was scary, if I'd worked for so long to keep it hidden, why on Earth would I choose to write about it in a national newspaper? I know that a lot of people think I'm crazy. No one was holding a gun to my head; no one was forcing me to do it. Or why not publish it anonymously? Curiously enough, this only occurs to me now: at the time I didn't even consider using a different name.

Something must have driven me, but I don't know what it was. Is everyone confessional these days; are we all compelled to spill our guts? An idea is planted and begins to grow, and then takes on a life of its own. Even as I was writing that first article for *The Times*, a few months before the weekly column began, I wasn't sure I'd actually publish it. Imagine telling the world, "I'm an alcoholic," "I'm impotent," "I binge-eat"—whatever your secret problem might be. It makes you feel horribly exposed. And one thing's for sure—coming out isn't as liberating as they tell you.

Far from it being cathartic, I found the whole process pretty disorienting. But this is a health crisis that matters on a larger scale. Like they say, the personal is political—and nowhere is this truer than with women and their weight. Yes, I was tired of anorexia, but I was also angry; I wanted to raise the issue of eating disorders and get it onto the public agenda (however modestly).

Of course it was my personal manifesto for recovery—a way of forcing my own hand—but that wasn't the only reason I wrote it. In some ways I'd have been happy to keep it between me, my family, and my psychiatrist, but I spoke out because I believe this is a much wider problem.

* * *

For too long, anorexia has been dismissed as a silly female hang-up, or something that affects only teenage girls: the quest for the perfect figure. But it isn't a lifestyle choice, it's a killer. The facts are bleak. Anorexia has a higher mortality rate than any other mental illness: up to 20 percent of sufferers will die, either from medical complications or suicide. Even if you don't die, it can wreck your bones and your fertility. For so-called "recovering" anorexics, the relapse rate is high. The U.K.'s leading eating disorders association, Beat, estimates that around 46 percent of anorexic patients go on to recover fully, with 33 percent improving, and another 20 percent remaining chronically ill. A less than 50 percent recovery rate? That's a shocking outcome compared to other conditions and their modern-day treatments. And as to 46 percent recovering "fully"—really? From my own experience, and having talked to many former anorexics, I believe you never completely get over anorexia. It's a deep scar, a mindset that stays with you for life, no matter how "normally" you learn to eat, no matter how well you learn to live with it.

And yet it's still not a public health priority. The "size zero debate" isn't really a debate at all. Compared to illnesses such as lung cancer or heart disease, eating disorders rarely figure on the political agenda. (The reason I mention these conditions is that they too may appear to be self-inflicted in some way, or the "fault" of the sufferer, like anorexia.) Where is the funding for research, where are the health initiatives? Why, when we know that psychological therapies can be of real benefit, are patients with eating disorders left for many months on waiting lists before they can get help?

Because it doesn't matter enough. The only recent intervention I can recall, at policy level, is the politician Lynne Featherstone's comments about curvy women in the TV series *Mad Men*. It's still on the BBC website.

"Christina Hendricks is absolutely fabulous" says Equalities Minister Lynne Featherstone, who held up Hendricks' outline as an ideal shape for women.

Highlighting the "over-exposure" of skinny models and the impact they have on body image among young people, Ms Featherstone went on: "We need more of these role models. There is such a sensation when there is a curvy role model. It shouldn't be so unusual." (BBC News, July 2010)

Cue many inches of newsprint analyzing Christina Hendricks's shape—is she size 14, size 16?—and her generous bosom, reportedly GG. Of course the media love this kind of sound bite—they show some close-ups of Hendricks's cleavage and get another opportunity to pass judgment on women's bodies, but one might have hoped for more from a politician. Featherstone's pejorative reference to "skinny" women and her celebration of "curvy" role models is reductive, simplistic. It's precisely this kind of tactless language that, however unintentionally, fuels women's anxieties and insecurities about their bodies (as online readers of this story pointed out).

And as for saying, "her curves are fabulous"—it's hardly a serious way to address a health crisis, is it?

On the rare occasions that eating disorders *are* mentioned in the media, they are linked to a tragic death—usually a teenage girl—

or a female celebrity whom the trashy magazines have decided is getting too thin (after previously vilifying her for being too fat). But having a specific body shape—be it "curvy" or "skinny"—is not the same as having a mental illness. When eating disorders are discussed in public, it's often assumed that women are starving themselves because they want to look like supermodels. But anorexia is about much more than what body shape happens to be in vogue with fashion editors or designers (whose sample sizes are mostly unwearable by all but prepubescent girls). Many catwalk models look quite bizarre in real life, freakishly tall and thin—and that's not why most anorexics are starving themselves.

No, anorexia is more serious than that, and the true extent of the problem will never be known. While the terms "epidemic" and "silent killer" are thrown around too carelessly by the media, the fact is that we don't have accurate medical data because eating disorders *are* shameful and silent and often invisible. It's in the nature of the disease to remain hidden—particularly with bulimia or binge-eating, where sufferers may appear to eat normally in public, and often maintain a normal body weight.

Figures from the National Institute for Health and Clinical Excellence (NICE) (usually taken to be the most accurate) suggest that 1.6 million people in the U.K. are affected by an eating disorder. It is estimated that 10 percent have anorexia, 40 percent have bulimia, and the remainder fall into the category of ED-NOS (Eating Disorder Not Otherwise Specified), which includes binge-eating disorder.

However, these figures are based on the Department of Health's Hospital Episode Statistics, so they leave out the unreported cases where sufferers are not receiving professional help or have not been diagnosed. And even the official research isn't consistent: an NHS study in 2007 (the Adult Psychiatric Morbidity Survey) showed that up to 6.4 percent of adults displayed signs of an eating disorder. I recently read an article in which it was claimed that "75 percent of all American women endorse some unhealthy thoughts, feelings or behaviors related to food or their bodies" ("Seventy-five percent of Women Have Disordered Eating," PsychCentral.com, 23 April 2008). Seventy-five percent sounds high, but it depends on the definition of "disordered eating" (and it may not be far wrong when you consider the obesity crisis in the U.S.).

Whatever the true figures, eating disorders are life-threatening conditions. And they're affecting women disproportionately: of the 1.6 million sufferers estimated by NICE, only 11 percent are male. Since I started writing my *Times* column, I've been amazed how many women have admitted their own problems with emotional eating: that they use food as a way of rewarding or punishing themselves, that they're ravenous all the time, that they diet constantly and break their diets and have low self-esteem. I know them, you know them—you may well be one of them yourself. Not skeletal, not dying, maybe not even that thin. Anorexics and bulimics and overeaters and many others, whatever their actual weight, have this in common: a sense of shame about their appetite, a feeling of being out of control around food—anxiety about eating, guilt around every bite.

Most of these women don't appear on the official statistics. They're not hospital patients, they're "normal." I know I hid my anorexia from myself, from those closest to me, for as long as I could: it was only the radical weight loss that forced me to stop denying it. I can only imagine how much harder it must be to ask for help when you're frantically overeating in private, already filled with shame, or bingeing and then vomiting.

I don't want to tar all women with the same brush. I don't want to generalize from women just dieting to those like me with a serious mental illness: I do understand that wanting to drop a dress size isn't the same as anorexia. In fact I wish it hadn't been necessary to raise the issue at all, but the situation is getting worse, not better: many of us experience body hatred (or mild dislike) every day. Images of beauty are becoming more idealized and bizarre; some of our most famous female celebrities look like Barbie dolls. The routine airbrushing of models and actresses in magazines gives boys and men a wholly distorted view of the female body as slim with huge breasts, perfectly toned and tanned, smooth and flawless.

I'm no more or less susceptible than any other woman. In terms of withstanding media pressure I'd say I'm quite robust: I know how to Photoshop an image and I'm pretty savvy about the artifice behind it all. I don't bother reading gossip magazines (unless I'm in a supermarket queue or at the hairdresser) and I've never aspired to look like those celebrities, all hair extensions and laser-whitened teeth. Sure, I shave my legs and I pluck my eyebrows and I wear makeup and perfume and deodorant. But I can't escape the madness around me, the impossible demands being put on women, to be thin, sexy, fertile, beautiful.

We're surrounded by these unrealistic images in magazines, on television and cinema screens. The perma-tans, the hairless limbs (why have women starting waxing their arms?) and wrinkle-free foreheads. Surely I'm not the only one who scans through interviews with well-known women to check their ages, who wonders how they managed to bear children, or whether they ever eat. Why do I do that?

In a much-reported interview in 2006 to launch her beachwear line, the celebrity Elizabeth Hurley revealed that she ate just one meal and precisely six raisins a day in order to keep her figure slim enough for her signature skintight white jeans (she owns over thirty pairs). To be counting out raisins in your early forties strikes me as slightly sad, but who am I to judge?

Even the least girly and most cynical among us notices the difference between "them" and us; how perfect they are and how imperfect we are. Really, how are we supposed to feel about ourselves, when we are human, with the natural sag of skin or the stretch marks of pregnancy, maybe a touch of cellulite on our thighs, all pasty from the British winter?

Even my bookish boyfriend lingers on the photographs of beautiful women in magazines, turns the page more slowly when there's a pretty actress—of course he does, it's a natural response. As an enlightened feminist, I hesitate to admit this, but it hurts. You want to say, "They don't really look like that," or "That's airbrushing," but of course that would be ridiculous. I'm sure Tom doesn't compare my flawed body to their sublime perfection; really, he loves me for who I am. But still, these are the digitally enhanced expectations of femaleness that boys and men see all around them. What a let down our naked bodies must be.

Even outside the unreal world of celebrity, where appearance is everything, the same thing is happening to high-profile women in the media. Look at the broadcasters, look at the female reporters. The *Countryfile* presenter Miriam O'Reilly was controversially sacked from the BBC in 2011 for being too old: she was fifty-three. (Of course I should add that she successfully sued for age discrimination, and is now back on the BBC.) There are still intelligent older women out there with gravitas—Anna Ford, Joan Bakewell, Kate Adie—but they themselves have spoken about the pressure to hold onto their positions. And I've noticed that they appear more often on radio than television these days.

* * *

Is this a feminist issue? Of course it is. Yes, there's pressure on men to smarten up their act, but nothing like the same degree. Look at

Jeremy Paxman, Andrew Marr, or Kenneth Clark. None of them is a work of art—you might even say they are succumbing to the ravages of time—and yet they are held in high regard for their intellect and experience. Look at Boris Johnson, our philandering, shambolic mayor of London. He makes a virtue of his scruffy appearance, all schoolboy hair and crumpled shirts, and women find it charming. I myself find Boris quite sexy. Mature male actors, broadcasters, and politicians can be overweight and graying, whereas women are over the hill at forty-five—or is it thirty-five these days? And why *is* Bruce Forsyth, in his eighties, hosting *Strictly Come Dancing* with the ex-model Tess Daly, who is half his age? Or more to the point, why isn't he hosting the show with a cohost in her eighties?

As a woman in her early thirties, I find it difficult. No woman can escape the pressure not to be frumpy or overweight, never to age (and how much harder must it be for teenage girls these days). Women are judged on their looks, men are not: that's why the personal is political.

There are countless examples of the objectification, the sexism—sometimes close to hatred—of women and their bodies. Recently, while researching an article for *Grazia* magazine, I asked a few female friends in their fifties and sixties what kind of journalism they wanted to read, what they were interested in and concerned about. The answer came back: *getting old and getting fat.*

As well as the media's obsession over weight, the latest thing is pregnancy scrutiny: whether the baby bump is too large or too small or just right. To me, this is an extension of the same old sexism: a judgmental attitude about women's bodies and shape. A recent interview with Mariah Carey opened with the male journalist commenting, "She's much larger in real life than in her airbrushed album shot" (he neglected to mention that the singer was pregnant with twins). There's the idiotic requirement to look glamorous (in five-inch heels) well into the final trimester; then the stern assessment of how quickly women lose their baby weight. "I just snapped back into shape" is what we hear from underwear models, back on the catwalk modeling bikinis three weeks after giving birth (with no pain relief, at home, in the bath). For weeks before the 2011 Royal Wedding, the media gleefully reproduced images of the "shrinking" Kate Middleton, feigning concern and speculating on a possible eating disorder, although no such scrutiny was given to the premature hair loss of her future husband. There were numerous web pages devoted to the question *Is Kate Middleton Anorexic?* The daily, casual sexism is so pervasive that we've gotten used to it—we've internalized the message that our value is bound up with our attractiveness. The message is clear: women's appearance is fair game, whereas men's doesn't really matter.

Jennifer Aniston, in her early forties, is regularly portrayed as a sad singleton, unable to keep the same man for very long, her bikini figure closely measured on her "lonely dog walks" along Santa Monica beach. (Maybe she's just walking the dog!) Meanwhile George Clooney, a good ten years older, is seen as a carefree bachelor. And when it comes to youth and beauty, women are caught in a catch-22. If they have cosmetic surgery they are ridiculed—the procedures are shocking and the results often horrendous.

But wait, surely cosmetic surgery empowers women? It gives them the breasts or the nose or the thighs they always dreamed of, right? No. It's not about reshaping or refining, it's violence dressed up as choice. Why are these women paying thousands of dollars to men in white coats to have their noses broken, their cheekbones sawn down, their jaws clamped and stomachs stapled, their eyelids sliced and hairlines lifted? Have you seen the bleeding and the bruising, have you read about the fluid loss, the skin ulceration and infection, the nerve paralysis? I don't think there's anything sadder than those stretched, painful, frozen expressions. Scalpels and Botox—cutting and poison. How did it get so bad for women?

The fact is, women aren't having cosmetic surgery to stay beautiful. As Naomi Wolf wrote in *The Beauty Myth* more than twenty years ago, many women who undergo surgery are fighting to stay loved, relevant, employed, admired; they're fighting against time running out. If they simply age naturally, don't diet or dye their hair, we feel they've "let themselves go." But if they continue to dress youthfully we feel they're "trying too hard" or brand them as "slappers." Poor Madonna, who has dared to be in her fifties. In order not to look like a woman in her sixth decade of life she exercises furiously, and is sniggered at by trashy magazines for having overly muscular arms and boytoy lovers. When Demi Moore's marriage to Ashton Kutcher, fifteen years her junior, recently broke down, the media reaction was almost gleeful. Of course, it was what they had been waiting for all along: how long could a forty-eight-year-old woman expect to keep a thirty-three-year-old man? As allegations of his infidelity emerged, the Internet was flooded with images of Demi looking gaunt and unhappy—and extremely thin.

Sometimes you want to say: just leave them alone. Then again, it's mostly women who buy these magazines, and women who write the editorials and online comments and gossip columns, so you could say we're our own worst enemies. There is already plenty of ageism and sexism out there—why do we add to the body hatred?

* * *

To me, the woman who exemplifies the modern female conundrum is Victoria Beckham. Don't laugh—I find myself weirdly fascinated by Posh Spice! She's a few years older than I am, and the Spice Girls were the hottest group when I was a teenager in the 1990s. I remember Victoria then, plumper than she is now and smiling in a miniskirt, getting engaged to David Beckham. I watched as she lost weight, got pregnant—those ridiculous wedding costumes (the start of the *OK!* and *Hello!* wedding industry)—had another baby, and another, getting thinner year by year.

What is Victoria so famous for? As she herself admits, she can't sing in tune—and I have no clue how much of her eponymous fashion line she designs herself. I don't know if I admire her or identify with her, or if I'm just curious. I can't remember a time when she wasn't in *Heat* magazine, or a time without the constant media updates on her weight loss, weight gain, weight anything. There were the unfortunate breast enlargements, the allegations of David Beckham's affairs. And yet she's still going. I don't care if she never smiles for the paparazzi (would you?), and I think she's genuinely pretty. I like the fact that she and David are still married and seem to be happy together; I like the fact that they're always out with their children.

Most of all, I'm fascinated by the pregnancies. She recently gave birth to her fourth baby: how does she do it? I'm the same height and weight as Posh. I know that every woman's reproductive system is different, but let me tell you—you're unlikely to ovulate naturally at that weight. I don't understand how she can conceive and carry a baby. How is that possible? (*Masses of fertility drugs and a large dollop of IVF* is what one doctor-friend told me— although of course that's just his opinion.) Faced with the necessity to gain weight in order to have a baby, I feel envious at her Earth Mother act; more than that I feel inadequate and frustrated. How come Posh gets to stay thin and elegant, when normal women have to have a certain level of body fat?

Speaking of fat, Victoria's eating habits are a particular source of media frenzy: there's an entire industry devoted to it. Apparently she'll only eat fish and steamed vegetables; apparently she's eating only pineapple now; apparently she takes a small set of scales into restaurants and weighs her food; apparently she cuts each portion in half and sends the other half back to the kitchen. Who knows whether it's fact or entirely media fiction—but the messages about food, body shape, and diet are certainly very confusing.

A photographer ex-boyfriend of mine once told me that the most lucrative paparazzi shots are those either up a woman's skirt—the so-called "money shot" (when she's getting out of the car, or falling out of a nightclub)—or a female celebrity eating. "It's really good if she's not wearing knickers, and even better if she's eating a hamburger."

* * *

Basically, when it comes to women, both aging and eating are somehow shameful. That sounds extreme, but it's true. And if you can't age and you can't eat, living is rather difficult. More than forty years after Germaine Greer published *The Female Eunuch*, a woman's worth is still very often measured by how she looks rather than by what she does. Just this morning I read a profile in *The Observer* of Christine Lagarde, the recently elected head of the International Monetary Fund; it focused more on her sex appeal, piercing blue eyes, and long legs than it did on her powerful new role. Lagarde is in her early fifties and likes designer clothes—so what? It doesn't seem to matter if men have wrinkles or gray hair—think Brad Pitt, Tom Cruise, Robert Redford. We don't care how old they are, or scrutinize their thighs for signs of cellulite, or juxtapose pictures of them with and without beer bellies on the beach.

Most of all, we don't gasp over pictures of famous men tucking into their food. This obsession with what women really eat is exemplified by the recent phenomenon of DIPE. DIPE is an acronym (coined in Hollywood) that stands for "Documented Instance of Public Eating." It's actually pretty funny: in any interview with a high-profile actress or model, DIPE is the emphasis on her large and healthy appetite—the way the interviewer spends the first paragraph describing the huge plate of pasta or bacon sandwich she orders. In a weird inversion, after years of being ladylike and terrified of appearing greedy in public, the image of the ravenous woman wolfing down her food has now become a sexualized one. Despite wanting women to be slim, men prefer women who enjoy their food. Women on diets are such a bore. So now women have to watch their weight and yet not appear to be watching their weight. And DIPE, all this tucking into fried chicken and burgers, is code for "I'm just a normal girl—I have a really fast metabolism, a huge appetite, and a great body." Of course it's a calculated strategy of image-crafting, and of course it depresses real women even more, because if we ate fried chicken and burgers we'd just get fatter. As my ex informed me, a hamburger shot of a pretty actress sells around the world (Penélope Cruz eats one after every Oscars ceremony).

No matter how secure you are, this is the world we inhabit today; for most women it's impossible to ignore. Of course the reasons for eating disorders are more complex and individual than this, but celebrity culture, the cosmetic surgery industry, and downright sexism cannot be ignored. Why else would this be an overwhelmingly female condition? Despite the worrying rise in male sufferers—I know men with eating disorders, and I know that the 11 percent statistic matters—the other 89 percent are women.

As a seventeen-year-old, when I first started reading about women's liberation, sexism and female inequality, women's bodies and hunger, work and motherhood, a whole new world opened up to me. Those feminist icons who changed my views on what it means to be a woman—Germaine Greer, Betty Friedan, Naomi Wolf, Susie Orbach—they were angry and articulate. They wrote that "the personal is political" and I liked the sound of it. It's only now that I begin to understand it.

How ironic, then, that for all my feminist principles and independence, growing up in a family of strong women, I should end up with anorexia, this most enfeebling of conditions.

Chapter 5

Heartbreak and the
Seeds of Anorexia

I say I don't know where anorexia came from, but that's not quite correct. I know what triggered it at the age of nineteen, but what I'll never fully understand are the underlying reasons. Why would I become anorexic, for example, when my sisters and school friends didn't? Almost everyone has problems and preoccupations growing up; some people become addicted to alcohol, drugs, or self-harm—but most don't. So why did I turn to starvation as a way of coping? It reminds me of that line in the 1980's film *The Breakfast Club*: "What's your poison?" Maybe I was genetically predisposed to getting an eating disorder, or maybe it's just a matter of temperament and circumstances, who knows? Certainly I have an addictive personality—I've always gotten hooked on things quickly.

I'm conscious, as I write this, of how lucky I've been, relatively speaking. Compared to many, my experience of anorexia has been bearable. From the outside at least I've lived a normal life. My weight was dangerously low for a while but I got through (and I never want to go back there again). Even though anorexia has affected every area of my life for more than ten years, I'm fortunate that it was "late-onset." It did not rob me of my childhood or adolescence—whatever happens in the future, at least I can say that. I know a girl, Sukey, who developed anorexia and bulimia at the age of eight. She is now twenty-four and in many ways she's still a child. She has never had a period or worn a bra, never had a boyfriend. The fear of puberty so often misattributed to anorexia is, in Sukey's case, very real. For her, any weight gain at all is associated with having a woman's body; she is stuck at the physical stage of around eight years old, with brittle bones and a wizened, old-lady face. She is the saddest person I've ever seen. So I'm aware of how lucky I am: although I've struggled with anorexia since the age of nineteen, at least I was a happy child and teenager; at least I remember all the wild times and the fun stuff, being carefree about food and relationships, getting drunk and eating kebabs and having curves and feeling sexy. At least I haven't always been this neurotic.

So if I was normal and healthy growing up, where did the anorexia come from? Picture an iceberg partially submerged under the sea, half sticking out above the water. Imagine the upper portion is your public persona, the face you show to the world. For that part, I'm fine. Below the surface, though, the underlying half of the iceberg, I'm a total mess. It doesn't have to be an iceberg—you can picture a building with shaky foundations, or a bicycle with loose wheels—but you get the general idea. There seems to be nothing solid inside me to hold it all together: in testing times, I fall apart; when something goes wrong, I turn on myself.

When I refer to "foundations" I don't mean childhood: I couldn't have had a more secure start in life. My parents' marriage is solid as a rock, and I've always been close to my family. School days were fine, as was adolescence. There was no specific trauma, no cruelty or catastrophe I can think of that might account for my later struggles.

What makes it harder to explain is that I'm genuinely a confident person—in many ways, I feel good about myself. Early on, my psychiatrist diagnosed me with *atypical* anorexia because I don't have the classic "distorted" view common to many anorexics. On the contrary, I'm well-informed about the physical, biological, and cognitive aspects of this condition. I've worked in psychology publishing for the last ten years. I understand the health risks. I see how self-defeating it is.

There's a well-known image of anorexia, a very thin woman looking in a mirror and seeing an obese woman looking back at her. That's not me. I'm thin, and when I look in the mirror, I see a thin woman looking back at me.

So this illness is not straightforward: I can't blame a simple lack of confidence. The top portion of my iceberg is outgoing and lively. For example, I'm fine about public speaking; I've read at weddings, I've given countless work presentations—after the initial nerves, I quite enjoy it. I've never felt that fear of "walking into a room," I'm happy to meet strangers, I don't even mind job interviews. I've traveled alone since I was a teenager, and I'm not fazed by going to the movies on my own. I think family, friends, colleagues would say I'm good company. Like most people I know, I should listen more and talk less, but I'm fun to be with—if not for dinner, then at least for drinking or a party.

It's what's underneath that needs work. Compliments, promotions—sure they happen; like anyone else, I've had my achievements. But for me success is like water off a duck's back; I somehow can't hold onto the glow. And then as soon as I get a hint of rejection, that's it. I castigate myself for trying, I hate myself for failing. I tell myself how stupid I was ever to have thought I might get anywhere. It's really unpleasant, how instantly I turn on myself, in ridicule and disgust. I replay the attempt or event—the relationship that went wrong, a scene at the office—

and wonder how I could have been so blind. *Did I not see all along that it wasn't going to work out? Did I honestly think I had a chance at getting that job? Didn't I notice that man didn't want me?*

I've never been able to take a positive view of failure. I can't believe in Samuel Beckett's words, "Ever tried, ever failed. No matter. Try again, fail again, fail better" (although that quote is stuck on my kitchen cupboard). I've never personally found much solace in those Pollyanna-platitudes: "It's all good experience" and "You learn from your mistakes." I struggle to see the positive side. It's not that I want to "win." Just that I feel so bloody awful about myself when I fail.

Remember that relationship book and film that came out a few years ago, *He's Just Not That Into You*? That title encapsulated everything I'd always suspected about myself, deep down.

I know I'm not the only one. Many confident people are chronically insecure; even high-flyers often say they feel like frauds, that they live in fear of being "found out." This profound sense of inadequacy is common—and one's actual worth or talent bears little resemblance to how one feels about oneself. In fact, I think the cleverest people must be pessimistic, depressed, because they are realistic, and they see how the world really is.

It all comes down to temperament, and I think this may be inherited. My mother and I are very similar in this: when we're rejected or ignored for any reason (a polite "no" from a publisher, a party we're not invited to) we immediately assume it's our fault. Our own standards (appearance, thinness) are too high, and we take setbacks or failures as a judgment on ourselves. Is it narcissistic to take life so personally?

Actually, I don't think it's narcissism. I think I just feel things too deeply, or take them too personally. Surely that's insecure rather than narcissistic?

Tom is the absolute opposite: he is constitutionally hopeful. Say he emails an editor pitching an idea for a newspaper article, and doesn't receive a reply for weeks, he'll happily say, "Oh, they're probably on vacation." I've quizzed him about this many times to try and understand his thought process: does he doubt himself? Does he blame himself for failure? He says that most of the time, it's not failure, just "crap circumstances." In other words, he doesn't internalize the rejection. When he doesn't receive a reply he genuinely believes that the editor is away or busy. He doesn't rush to the conclusion that his writing is rubbish, or they don't want *him*.

And yet personality is never simple. When it comes to me, to my feelings for him, Tom is much less secure. He is convinced that any male acquaintance of mine must be either an ex-boyfriend or a prospective suitor, and at times he has driven us both to despair with his accusations and suspicions. For all my anorexic craziness, this level of jealousy is something I can't relate to—I've never felt it or understood it. If someone wanted to cheat on me, either he would or he wouldn't; but, in either case, what good would imagining it do me? Why would you want to spend your life with one person and be unfaithful? When we discuss it rationally, Tom understands this, but emotions are not always rational, I know. We both have elements of confidence and insecurity—sensitivities, weaknesses—I'm sure that's true of us all. Tom feels secure about work but not about me, as if something deep down refuses to believe in my love. I don't suffer these torments of emotional jealousy—I feel secure in his love—but I experience daily doubts in my own abilities and in myself as a person. I'm almost in despair from the moment I send out an idea into the world, and I spend most of my life expecting the next failure.

So I'm confident in some ways and an insecure wreck in others, like lots of people; so what's the big deal? What has any of this to do with anorexia? I think it's about resilience. When things go wrong, as they always will, for all of us, you need that inner core. You need to believe, fundamentally, that you're OK. You need to have faith in yourself. But I don't. I have no ballast, so whenever life gets tricky or when I fall short, I flounder.

I have thought about this a lot. What it comes down to is a total lack of self-belief.

* * *

Anorexia started as a response to a major breakup. I was nineteen years old, and from that point on I've basically been at war with myself.

If you've been telling yourself for years that (deep down) you're a failure, then rejection, when it comes, isn't that surprising. But there are degrees of hurt. And however painful it is to be rejected for a job, to mess up an exam or fail your driving test, nothing comes close to rejection in love.

It's strange, this one, love and relationships and breakups. I hear people saying it's not personal; you shouldn't take it personally. This seems madness. If it's a serious relationship, how can it be anything but intensely personal? Someone has fallen in love with you, shared their secrets, gotten to know your body and your mind, bathed with you, slept beside you, tasted your skin and sweat and tears—and then they say, "You're not for me." When a relationship ends, of course you can't blame anything but yourself.

I've had lots of boyfriends and experienced plenty of endings, both as the dumper and the dumpee. In fact, I was usually the one calling time on relationships, but of course I only ever remember the other ones: I can recall with absolute clarity the occasions when I have been chucked—the humiliation—but my memories are hazy about all the others. Over the years, whenever I got dumped my mother would say, "It's not you, it's him." She's right about most things, but she's wrong about that. Of course it's about "you." It's outright rejection, what could be clearer? The precise meaning of a dumping is surely this: I don't love you. Or, I don't love you *enough*.

Come on, we all know the truth about love. When you're into someone, you'll do almost anything to be with them, uproot your home, sell your soul, climb mountains . . . When you're not, you just want to get free.

I had been lucky, I suppose, up to the age of nineteen. The odd setback, a failed driving test or two, but nothing to shake my foundations. On a failure-and-rejection scale of one to ten, if the driving tests were a three (I couldn't afford a car back then, and anyway it's impossible to park in London), the breakup I went through was an eleven.

I stop typing for a moment and take a swig of Diet Coke. I don't really want to go back to all this, but I want to be honest about what triggered my anorexia. For most of us there's been someone we'll love forever even though it didn't work out (or precisely because it didn't work out). You know the one who hurt you more than anyone ever did, the one you thought you couldn't live without? For me that person is Laurence.

The fallout from that relationship nearly wrecked my life. That's not a blame thing, it's just the truth.

* * *

As I try to piece together what happened in New York and Oxford, I realize that a failed love affair doesn't seem like a particularly logical reason to stop eating. OK, so my heart was all smashed up, but that happens to most people at some point in their lives.

Starving oneself is sort of an odd response, isn't it? I don't know why anorexia was the way I chose to punish myself, if I in fact chose it at all. But if you asked anyone who was close to me, they would say that after Laurence I was a different person: quieter, thinner obviously, but also withdrawn.

It's a hackneyed phrase but, compared to life before anorexia, I feel like a shadow of my former self. It is obvious to me, and obvious to others, that something in that relationship damaged me. Am I blaming Laurence? No. He was under no obligation to continue our relationship. He didn't know I would go on to develop an eating disorder. And anyway, cause and effect is never that straightforward. Probably the seeds of anorexia were sown much earlier than this, in my childhood or adolescence. So it's worth going back a few years, to explain who I was before anorexia came along.

I was a happy teenager, living in North London, attending the prestigious St. Paul's Girls' School. My big sister, Katie, and my little sister, Alice, attended the same school, and my two brothers, Philip and Tristram, went to St. Paul's Boys' School just across the Thames. The alumni of St. Paul's include John Milton and Samuel Johnson and George Osborne and Imogen Stubbs and Rachel Weisz and Harriet Harman: countless authors and politicians, musicians and actresses. The two schools are notorious for producing high-flying, high-profile, scarily confident young women and men. My A level year contained the following: Michael Howard's daughter, John Major's goddaughter, Charles Darwin's great-granddaughter, and a couple of Lord Sainsbury's nieces. Besides their lofty connections, St. Paul's girls were hilariously rich and spoiled. I remember my best friend's seventeenth birthday: her brand-new black convertible Range Rover was driven into Brook Green as we smoked illicit cigarettes outside the school gates.

Conversely, my family was hilariously poor. It may not sound like it—what with the private schooling—but my parents really were stony broke. They managed, miraculously, to do things on a shoestring: camping instead of hotels, picnics instead of restaurants, and all our school uniforms were hand-me-downs, altered and spruced up by my mother. And when the ancient Triumph Herald car broke down, again, and we had to be towed home, again, they made it seem like an adventure.

But even back in the 1980s and 1990s, when bursaries and scholarships were available (and we did benefit from financial assistance), I still don't know how my parents managed to put all five of us through the most expensive day schools in London. Our fees were paid, but then there was everything else: new textbooks, theater tickets, sports equipment, endless demands for money they must have struggled to meet. My brothers and sisters and I were interlopers in the midst of all that wealth.

I never went on the school trips: skiing in Verbier, archaeological digs in Greece, or lacrosse tours of China. As children we spent all our vacations in Europe—we'd load up the car and camper and "motor" to France and Italy. We would drive and drive and then park somewhere at night—not in a campsite but in a secluded turnout or a field of corn. Mum and Dad slept in the camper and the five of us slept in the car—two in the trunk, two on the backseat and one on the front seat. (Have you ever tried sleeping across a car hand brake?)

And I didn't get a convertible for my seventeenth birthday (although I did get a weekend job at Woolworth's). Katie, Philip, Alice, Trim, and I made our way from Camden Town to Hammersmith every day on the Northern and Piccadilly lines, a ragamuffin bunch of Woolfs, reading and arguing and eating Curly-Wurlies as we went.

These days St. Pauls's Girl's School is portrayed as a hotbed of eating disorders, but I don't remember it like that. No one seemed particularly thin or obsessive about her weight, or it may be I didn't notice, because back then I had no concerns about food. It's only fifteen or twenty years ago and yet it seems a different world. We just didn't have all the magazines and Internet images—there wasn't the intense scrutiny on every aspect of women's bodies, faces, hair, teeth, bunions, nails, wrinkles, skin color, tone, cellulite. Botox didn't exist—and getting a facelift was something mad old Hollywood actresses did at the age of ninety-five.

In a world without *Heat* or *Closer*, we read our favorite magazines, *Just Seventeen* and *Mizz*, religiously. The articles were all about sparkly eyeshadow and how to dance like Madonna— not diets or fitness regimes or how much women weighed. Once in a while we borrowed a copy of *Vogue* from someone's mum, but the models weren't as thin as they are now. Remember the "supers": Cindy Crawford with the mole and Linda Evangelista with her brightly colored hair! As I remember it, we talked about our boyfriends, we smoked Silk Cut, we avoided double lacrosse and we terrorized our chemistry teacher.

I don't remember anyone skipping lunch, getting super-thin, or over-exercising; I don't remember any anorexic talk. Weirdly, in a recent session with my psychiatrist, I recalled sitting in the locker rooms at St. Paul's: it was morning break, I was with a group of friends, and we were all eating Mars Bars and sipping styrofoam cups of coffee from the vending machine. Then I remembered one of the girls stood up and went into the bathroom, and I heard her retching. She had been perfectly fine until that moment, and when she came out she asked who wanted to go for a cigarette. I now suppose she had bulimia, but did I understand that at the time?

With A levels over, and a place at Oxford to study English Literature, I went to Paris for the summer with my best friend. It was the end of school and the beginning of the rest of our lives: we criss-crossed the bridges of Paris, read Camus, stayed up all night, drank a lot of wine.

In September I came back to London and worked full-time in Woolworth's until Christmas. I was by this time "Head of Entertainment," which meant I had to rearrange all the cassettes and CDs of the Top 40 Chart before the shop opened every Sunday morning—when I had a raging hangover.

With a bit of money in the bank, I could begin my year off before university. On New Year's Eve I boarded a flight for New York. It seems strange to me now, but I had never been on a plane before.

* * *

Age eighteen, I landed at JFK and that's where it all began. My big sister, Katie, five years older than I am, was living in New York and had invited me to come and stay for a few weeks. She met me at the airport and we took the subway home, got dressed up, and hit the first of the New Year parties. At ten minutes to ten (it was party number two or three, they were handing out sambuca shots at the door) I ran into Laurence.

This wasn't our first meeting. In fact, I'd known Laurence—we called him Laurie—since the age of thirteen when he used to visit London with his parents. He was a year older than I. His mother and my mother are close friends, both writers and academics, my mother at London University, his mother at New York University, and they often stay with each other during conferences or research trips.

With my newly rediscovered big sister and Laurie and a gaggle of friends, I reeled from party to party. Despite the alcohol and the jet lag, I have quite clear memories of that first night in Manhattan. I remember a lively Chinese meal (how odd, that I could eat in public back then); I remember standing outside the restaurant on Broadway with Laurie, sharing a cigarette. I remember various cab rides, criss-crossing from the Upper West Side to the Upper East Side; I remember a rooftop party at midnight, the music and fireworks, looking out over the Hudson River, and our first kiss.

I don't know how to describe our relationship: inevitably the pain that followed has clouded much of the happiness we experienced at the time. But as for New York—it captured my heart. There is a line in *Heartburn* by Nora Ephron that reminds me of that time in my life and the excitement of discovering the city, about how New Yorkers are always rushing around "looking for action, love, and the world's greatest chocolate chip cookie." I had planned to stay a fortnight, and ended up staying for nearly a year. I got a job (in advertising), a shoebox apartment (on the Upper East Side), and fell in love (for the first time). I ate plenty of chocolate chip cookies.

* * *

Why did I fall for Laurie so badly? It wasn't my first serious relationship. I had lost my virginity at the age of seventeen to a very nice chap called Jamie who went to St. Paul's. We met at the joint Poetry Discussion Group—which is where the girls went to meet boys and vice versa. He declared his intentions at the Christmas party at Twickenham Rugby Club; I remember it still, liking someone so much, praying he liked me back.

We were both virgins, and after dating for months we decided the time was right. Virginity was threatening to become a burden—sixteen was the age to lose it, seventeen was considered the cut-off point in those days. I was seventeen and a half and

Jamie was nearly eighteen. We borrowed his aunt's cottage in Devon for the weekend and did the deed. To be honest, it was more fumbling than passionate, but it was a relief to have gotten it over with. Afterward we went outside and sat on the sea wall; I remember Jamie was crying and I was thinking about how much it had hurt.

So, Laurie wasn't the first in that sense. But it was my first proper adult relationship: we were practically living together, and I was 3,500 miles from home. According to Laurie "it had been on the cards for years" (to me, his arrogance was part of his charm), and neither of us felt the need to pretend. That was new, the emotional openness and physical intimacy. At school our relationships had been immature; being cool was more important than being honest. If someone fancied you, or was about to dump you, you adjusted your feelings accordingly. Laurie and I never hid our feelings from each other: we were in love and heading in the same direction.

Our relationship was inevitable: the shared family history, and the tension that had been building in those too-brief meetings as teenagers; we got on pretty well as adults too. There was a genuine intellectual connection and shared interests: literature, languages, travel. We were competitive as hell—I would study at Oxford and he at Cornell. Unlike most Americans, Laurie had traveled widely in Europe; he spoke fluent French, Italian, and German. And, unlike my disappointment on that sea wall in Devon, sex with Laurie was irresistible. He wasn't conventionally gorgeous—very tall, lanky, floppy brown hair—but urbane, handsome. He dressed like the privileged Jewish New Yorker he was, with an academic antistyle thing going on (picked up in Europe, I think), all crumpled shirts and corduroys. He was the first vegan I'd ever met, and we spent hours discussing the rights of animals. I'd always been uncomfortable with the idea of eating dead animals—my mother recalls me as a child sitting for hours over a plate of whitebait: I couldn't bring myself to put those tiny silvery fish in my mouth. Now, independent and free to make my own food choices, it all made sense. I never went as far as Laurie's strict veganism—I wear leather shoes, for example, and drink milk—but I have not eaten meat or fish to this day.

Nothing lasts forever. I had to leave New York and come back to start my degree. I remember saying goodbye to Laurie at the departures gate at JFK: I remember my anxiety for him; it seemed unthinkable that we could survive apart. There was no doubt in either of our minds that we were going to stay together across the Atlantic. We wrote constantly, long letters and postcards, and sent each other faxes daily. We signed up for long distance telephone deals—only 20 cents a minute to the U.S.—and we got email accounts back when they were quite the newest technology.

Ten weeks later, as we were planning our reunion—I was going to fly out to New York for Christmas, then Laurie would fly back with me for New Year's in Oxford—I received an airmail letter out of the blue. He said this long-distance thing "wasn't working," that he needed a girlfriend who was around, that it was better for both of us to make a fresh start, alone.

The hurt was indescribable. I stayed in my college room for five days straight. I remember I drank water straight from the tap and sat on the floor by the window smoking duty-free U.S. cigarettes. I didn't go out to lectures or to the shops (it was the first time in my life I'd gone without food). I don't remember crying, just feeling completely blank—I couldn't get my mind around living without him. Then I took a shower, unlocked the door, and set about destroying myself.

Chapter 6
Things Fall Apart

How can I describe those years in Oxford? I won't begin with the beauty of the "dreaming spires" or gambling trips down the River Cherwell (I'm no poet, and anyway it's been done much better in *Brideshead Revisited*). Nor will I go on about the books I read and essays I wrote, the inspiring lectures and the libraries, the University Parks, the lanes and colleges and pealing bells . . . They are all locked up inside, woven into my memories of Oxford, but they are not part of this story.

Those three years, from the ages of nineteen to twenty-one, should have been a time of growth; instead they were a time of shrinking, of near collapse. And yet I remember them as happy. It strikes me now as strange, that I was colder and hungrier than I'd ever been in my life, but I remember being happy.

The spark that had been ignited by the end of my relationship with Laurie caught fire. With my fundamental lack of self-belief, I blamed myself. I turned the pain inward; I despised myself for getting rejected, so punishment was the next logical step. I believe this is what self-harmers do: cut themselves on the outside in order to relieve the pain inside. I understand the impulse very well, although I have never deliberately injured myself. (I write this, and then a few days later I receive an email from a psychiatrist who reminds me that "anorexia is also a form of self-harm." God, that makes me feel uneasy.)

Starving myself was a way of coping with the pain I felt, and a way of controlling myself. Clearly I was too much for Laurie. Too talkative, too emotional, too fleshy. In short, too fat. I believed this, despite the fact that I was average height and weight, slap bang in the "normal" section of the BMI charts. Photographs of me aged nineteen show I had a nice figure.

I had no way of dealing with my emotional chaos, so I found a physical solution. Of course none of this was clear to me then, but I wasn't thinking straight. I was thinking about Laurie all the time. The overwhelming feeling was one of abandonment and humiliation. I hated myself, not him. (I've never been able to hate him.)

Self-starvation does a good job of muting everything. When you're eating so little, you don't have any reserves left over to get emotional or dramatic about life; mine became a pretty low-level existence. And yet it's also hard work: being constantly hungry requires focus; you mustn't slip up and eat something, you mustn't give in and show that you need food or a hug; you mustn't allow your appetite to get the better of you. You don't deserve to eat.

When anorexia starts, it's like any normal diet. You lose weight gradually, steadily, a pound or two a week. It's satisfying to see your efforts pay off: a simple game of cost and reward. You resist the croissant or the brownie you used to have with a friend in a café, you drag yourself to the gym every morning, and it starts working. Fewer calories in, more calories out: the numbers on the scale go down. It really is that simple.

* * *

It may be simple in theory, but in practice it's not easy to stop eating. Human beings—even superhuman anorexics—are programmed to hunt, gather, and consume; calories are life and survival. It takes a lot of energy to overcome the natural impulse to eat, to deny yourself food every hour, every day, when you're constantly hungry. And this is one of the greatest misunderstandings about this disease—that anorexics don't like food. One of the questions I'm continually asked is: "So why don't you like food?" Really, truthfully, I don't hate food. (Fear, yes; hate, no.) I spend most of my life worrying about it; perhaps that's why I avoid it so assiduously.

What do I love? Oh, foods I haven't eaten for years: pasta shells drizzled with butter and grated Cheddar cheese, the butter collecting inside the shells; doorstep-thick whole-wheat toast loaded with chunky marmalade; tagliatelle and pesto; take-out fries in greasy newspaper covered in salt and vinegar; stir-fries and veggie curries and all Chinese food; freshly baked French bread torn off the baguette and eaten with wedges of melting brie and rough red wine; baked potatoes and baked beans; tacos and refried beans and enchiladas and seven-layer burritos from Taco Bell in Florida; the first new potatoes of the season, piping hot in garlic butter— the tasty, indulgent things we all love. Late at night, chocolate and peanut M&M's mixed up in colorful handfuls. The macaroni and cheese my mum used to make when we were little.

I'm amazed as I write this of the memories that flood back, the flavors I can almost taste, all the foods I might eat if there were no rules. And yet I'm detached as I remember them, because I can't imagine eating them ever again. I just can't countenance allowing myself to. I call them memories because it's so long since I tasted them. Sometimes I walk slowly past the Cornish pasty place in the tube station on a cold winter's day, and I want to faint with the smell that comes out (can smells make you fat?). Of course those are pasties and pies—I admit, I couldn't eat a pie in a million years—but when you're starving the pie smell (potato, cheese, crust) is so warm and delicious, so complex. I still remember how good fish and chips used to taste. As children, on family vacations, we'd share a large bag of fries in the backseat of the car, or on vacation at the seaside. The greasy bag, the salty, crispy potato wedges, the taste on one's lips, the warmth of food . . .

Looking back at what I've just written, I see that my favorite foods are simple, you might even say childish. It's as if I missed out on developing adult tastes because I developed anorexia just as I was becoming an adult.

"But what do you actually eat?" That's the other question everyone asks when you have an eating disorder. Fruit and vegetables mostly: apples, oranges, bananas, broccoli, asparagus, spinach. A lot of muesli and probiotic natural yogurt. Sometimes, for a treat, whole-wheat pita bread and low-fat hummus. More recently, perhaps buoyed up by the first days of spring, I've embarked on some new food experiments: Super Wholefood Couscous from Marks & Spencer, three-bean and tomato soup. Tom and I have been out in his garden, planting some April bulbs. New life, a new season—and it reminds me I have to stay focused on my challenge, I have to keep expanding my food horizons.

* * *

Back in Oxford, I was eating very little. For me, anorexia really did start like that: first just cutting out treats, then cutting out all fattening foods, then skipping entire meals—seeing the scales drop and my jeans getting looser. I was a mess of emotions I couldn't even start to acknowledge. Compared to the breakup, anorexia was bearable: the discomfort of being hungry all the time was nothing compared to the twisted pain in my heart. And anyway, I felt very badly in the wrong: I had been rejected and it was my fault. Not allowing myself to eat was a start.

I can't honestly trace the line between a diet and anorexia. There must be an invisible threshold, and I don't know when I crossed it. I suppose this is the heart of the matter: why most people can go on a diet (and either keep the weight off, or regain it) while others spiral into the madness of a full-blown eating disorder. All I know is that once it started, anorexia very quickly took off. In all the buried hurt and shame, it seemed I had found something that worked. I could control this. And the self-annihilation accelerated from that point on.

When I started university I weighed 133 pounds. When I left I weighed 77 pounds.

* * *

My memories from Oxford are broken and intense. When I look back, I can tell which year it was not from events or the actual date, but from the way I was feeling.

First year: party animal, lots of boyfriends, not much work, getting stoned on weekends with friends at Balliol and Corpus Christi, starting to lose weight, looking good. Second year: much thinner, joining the gym, a few close friendships, more alcohol than food. Third year: withdrawal into the library and my rooms, exercising obsessively, working constantly, reading, writing poetry, eating almost nothing, a lot of doctor's appointments.

That downward spiral—of my body, my mind, my grip on life—was visceral, unlike anything I've ever experienced. It's exhilarating and terrifying, watching everything fall apart. I had rigid control and no control. I don't know what I was thinking—I wasn't trying to starve myself to death; I don't remember a game plan as such. I didn't want to die, but I knew I was badly caught. I didn't know where it would end.

As well as feeling trapped, I was also in pain. With zero fat, either normal subcutaneous body fat or energy food fat, you're constantly fighting for survival. All anorexics speak of the cold, and I found those winters in Oxford unbelievably hard. Just now I checked the Met Office website out of curiosity, to see if the recorded temperatures for those three Decembers in the late 1990s were any lower than usual; of course they weren't. So why was I colder than I ever knew it was possible to feel?

I recall one night at a friend's birthday party at Maxwell's, a cocktail bar in the center of town. It was crowded with students and well-heated but the cold had penetrated my bones, and I simply had no insulation to keep me warm. I froze in a turtleneck and jeans and boots surrounded by friends in sleeveless tops and skimpy dresses. It had taken all my strength to come out, and I tried to stay, but I couldn't concentrate on any conversation and the tips of my fingers had gone numb. Finally I slipped out into the dark night and walked the two miles home alone along the main road. I could have taken a bus or a taxi, but that would have been "fat" behavior. Anorexia is a process of constant self-punishment: small everyday cruelties, an inability to be kind to oneself or to say, *You're tired, you're cold, just get into a warm cab.* Back in my flat at the student block on Iffley Road I ran the hottest bath I could stand. I still remember how it hurt to sit down, because my tail bone stuck out and grated against the bottom of the bath, and my elbows and knees were sharp against the sides. I was covered in livid bruises from the slightest knock. That night as I lay in the scalding water, pale and paper-light, I thought of my friends back in Maxwell's getting drunk on jugs of Sea Breeze. That was a turning point, of sorts, floating there, wondering how many more winters I could take.

* * *

After months of deceiving myself, deceiving the doctors, gaining and losing the same few pounds, I was driven to make the decision: I would have to try and put on some weight. Although I rarely looked at myself in the mirror anymore, I could see how sick I appeared. I was being seriously threatened with hospitalization. I was put on Prozac—more on that later. Though it wasn't immediate, gradually those little green-and-white pills began to even out the imbalanced chemicals in my brain. More than that, other people's concern was becoming intrusive. Their concern had gone from medium to severe: it was Code Orange now. With phone calls between my tutors and parents and friends, I began to work in my college rooms so I didn't have to face anyone. I was nearly twenty-one, for God's sake; I didn't want their concern. I needed to stay in Oxford, to take my finals. Gaining weight was the only way I could see to avoid the hospitals and keep control of my life.

Then one weekend in April, six weeks before the start of finals, two things happened. On Saturday evening, a visit from an ex-boyfriend, Steven. He was staying with his brother for a few days; we sometimes hooked up when we were unattached and both in London, or I was in Manchester, or he was in Oxford. We hadn't met up for six months or so, and I was aware (as I was all the time, horribly, during those years) that people I hadn't seen recently tended to be shocked at my weight loss. Steven was easygoing and we'd stayed fairly close since our relationship two years earlier: we'd have a few drinks, we'd end up in bed together, or just hang out, but it was no big deal. He arrived around 7 PM with a bottle of white burgundy and we lolled on my bed for a while, drinking wine and catching up. The radio was playing and "our song" came on: Al Green's "Let's Stay Together." We jumped up and decided to dance, for old times' sake and because we were tipsy. It's a slow dance, and it was nice just being close, barely moving, holding each other, and nice when Steve kissed me too.

After a minute or so, I put my hand up to his cheek and felt tears on his face. He was crying.

He wasn't kissing me out of lust or passion; all that was gone. Kind, sexy Steve put his arms around me and found nothing but a skeleton. I have tried to erase the words he said, but I can't forget the look in his eyes—a mixture of shock and sorrow. He asked what had happened to me and I said I was OK; Steve said I wasn't, and he left around midnight.

Stinging from this awfulness, I got up even earlier than usual on Sunday morning and crossed the road to the Iffley Road gym (where Roger Bannister ran the first ever four-minute mile). The gym was deserted. I plugged in my headphones and did my usual hour on the treadmill, then a couple of kilometers on the rowing machine. On the way out, the gym manager stopped me at the front desk and asked to have a word. They were sorry, he said, but they had decided to terminate my membership. It was on health grounds, he explained; they felt perhaps I was overdoing it, perhaps I should give my body a rest. They would of course refund my remaining months. I had never been so humiliated in my life.

* * *

So self-preservation, vanity, desperation, Prozac, pride? Whatever the reasons, and slowly—painfully slowly—I managed to gain some weight. That last summer in Oxford I stayed out of the hospital and took my finals and got a good degree. It was incredibly hard to start eating again, but as I did so, life got easier. (It's hard to imagine if your weight has never dipped that low, but every extra ounce makes an incredible difference to your state of mind and your well-being.)

I was still hovering around 90 pounds, but it was better than 77. I spent the summer traveling alone—Egypt, Italy—did some freelance work in London, had an interesting relationship with a psychology professor, and I kept on making myself eat. Bread, pasta, anything simple, unthreatening. Small amounts, but enough to keep going.

Every bite was bloody agony. Every time I thought about eating I felt greedy. I felt like I didn't deserve it. I felt like hell. But by the time I started my graduate job in an advertising agency that September, I was stable. I still looked pretty thin but I was out of the danger zone. I was back in the land of the living.

I stayed that way for years, just under 100 pounds. This is what "functional anorexia" means: you have a normal life, a career, a home; you maintain this alongside an eating disorder. I moved from working in advertising to publishing and began to find my niche. I rented a small studio flat in Camden Town, then I bought a one-bedroom flat in Elephant & Castle. It wasn't the most salubrious part of London, but I loved that little flat in a cul-de-sac just off the Bricklayers' Arms bridge. I remember the day the sale went through—a Tuesday morning at work, as usual. The purchase had dragged on for months, and my first brush with mortgage advisors and surveyors and solicitors had been the usual hassle, but finally the estate agent called, "The funds have cleared, the flat's yours. Come and collect the keys whenever you want."

I jumped on my bike instantly and cycled from my office in Euston to Borough High Street. The estate agent looked surprised to see me because he'd barely hung up the phone. I had the keys, the place was mine. I'd never been in there before, without the estate agent. Feeling like a burglar, I unlocked the front door. The flat was empty and filled with sunshine—just old wooden floorboards and bare white walls and a large fridge. I pulled the bottle of champagne I bought for the occasion out of my backback and plugged in the fridge and set the bottle to chill. I texted Nick, my boyfriend at the time (a Polish stunt cyclist), and my sisters:

I have keys! Come for bubbly at 7 PM*?* Then I cycled back to the office and got on with the rest of the afternoon.

(By the way, that's quite an interesting example of anorexia in action. Do you see what happened there? I'd been up at 6 AM and biked into work (five miles) and drank my black coffee and eaten my apple, and then maybe a banana midmorning, then I'd cycled over the flat at lunchtime—thereby avoiding any opportunity to eat, I'm always "too busy" to eat—then collected the keys, then cycled back to work, then cycled home at the end of the day, then showered and changed and drank champagne to celebrate . . . so, twenty miles cycling and a full day's work, all rushing and excitement and nothing to eat except fruit. That's how I lived back then—and some days, if I'm upset or busy or unsettled, I still do this now. If there's a choice between taking the tube and cycling, ideally somewhere far away and exhausting, I'll cycle. If there's a chance to miss a meal, I'll take it. Sometimes I don't even make the decision consciously; I'm hardwired that way. This is the way anorexia manifests itself: doing too much on too little—and always, always dodging food.)

I lived in that flat at Elephant & Castle for three years, during which time my weight remained fairly stable. My eating was far from normal—I barely ate in the office, rarely around other people, but my colleagues were used to me by now. I would join them in the pub on a Friday after work, but never for a sandwich in the park at lunchtime: alcohol was OK, food was not. There was a close bunch of us, all in our twenties, young editors and designers. I think I was seen as slightly reserved, aloof—or maybe I'm kidding myself. Maybe everyone knew I was anorexic and talked about me as the skinny one with food issues (I hope not). Anyway, those were happy years, working my way up in publishing.

As I became a more senior commissioning editor, I went out drinking less with my contemporaries anyway, so the food avoidance got easier. Unfortunately I also had to do more entertaining—taking authors out to lunch and so on. If you've ever thought that having an eating disorder is just confined to mealtimes, think again. Food permeates every part of our lives—our friendships and relationships (cooking for each other, family meals, treats) and work. I can't explain how difficult anorexia has made my career; almost every week there is another fearful event involving eating, a meeting with catered sandwiches, an office party, a birthday, a going-away party, or drinks and nibbles. And food is always involved and must always be avoided.

One particular work lunch sticks in my mind. It's years ago now, and I'm not sure why I remember this one with such clarity when every one of those simple business engagements involving food was traumatic. I had recently decided to put on weight and "give up anorexia"—another half-hearted attempt doomed to failure. But at the time, anyway, it was the first day of my new regime, another fresh start I'd been postponing for weeks. I was the Psychology Publisher by this point, and was taking a new author out for lunch. Normally I would have arranged to meet for coffee in a smart patisserie—and then buy lavish pastries to make up for it—but two senior colleagues were coming along too and had suggested a "first-class lunch." So I wasn't able to wriggle out of it.

We were booked into an Italian restaurant not far from the office. My anxiety had been building for weeks—the night before the lunch itself I didn't sleep at all. I must have checked the restaurant's website at least five times, scanning the menu to check for potential pitfalls and work out what might be safe. It was a beautiful winter's day, bright and crisp, the first sunshine London had seen in weeks. As we left the office, the editor who sat next to me, a lovely girl and a good friend, waved and said, "Hope the meeting goes well, Em—hey, at least it's a free lunch." This is something I heard all the time at work, and I never understood it.

People would say, "Oh no, bloody office party—I'm only going for the free food." It's a concept that has always amazed me—I'd do anything to avoid the free-food part of free work events: feign illness, climb out of a window, anything!

Every day at work I would see people going for lunch together, casually, happily. I would marvel at how uncomplicated it looked. Over the years I've done everything I could to avoid eating with others: I have smuggled bananas into stationery cupboards, eaten bread rolls in toilet stalls, eaten yogurts on park benches in the rain. If there are people around, if I can't find a place to be alone, I simply go without food.

And that's just the practical side—let alone the social side of things, the excuses, the evasions, and how bloody antisocial it seemed. I've made some really good friends over the years at work, but there's always been this barrier preventing me getting close to any of them. I know they find it strange. In offices, lunch is where friendships are formed and cemented, where casual workmates become allies: it's the only opportunity during the working day to escape and gossip about your evil boss or confide in each other. When I saw them all, congregating for lunch, I'd wonder why the hell I made it so difficult for myself. Wouldn't it be simpler and nicer to buy a real sandwich and eat it out in the open—on the grass in summer, or at my desk in the office, or in a sidewalk café? Or with friends? It's been years since I did that willingly.

Perhaps this explains my extreme foreboding of that lunch meeting. I remember how much I just wanted the meal to be over. We were seated at a round table in the window, all shining silverware and cream linen napkins. Then the author arrived: introductions were made, hands were shaken, and the waiter distributed menus. But I was ready, wasn't I? I knew what I was going to order—although there was always the risk that the menu had changed.

I recall the panic inside my head: it seemed insanely early to be sitting down to lunch; I was aghast at the thought of an entire meal. The anorexic voice seemed very loud in the hushed restaurant. Eating now—when you haven't even deserved it? Surely it's only the morning? It was 1:30 PM. I would normally have allowed myself a banana or an apple around that time—but a full cooked meal in a restaurant? Hot food at that time? Anyway, I ordered a Diet Coke and the author ordered an orange juice (he was driving) and my two colleagues ordered a bottle of red wine.

The waiter brought our starters (plain green salad for me) and we discussed the new book, and then he brought our main courses: steaks for them and pasta with arrabbiata sauce for me. It was a huge portion of spaghetti, which made me irrationally angry. It seemed so unfair that even if I ate fully half of the massive plateful, it would still look as though I wasn't eating properly. This upset me, just when I'd made the effort to act normal, and, more than that, it upset me because it was so much goddamn food. It tasted so good (I'd forgotten) and I was so hungry (I was constantly hungry) and all my fears about gluttony were confirmed, because I knew I could probably have eaten the entire portion of spaghetti three times over. Because the truth is: I'm a glutton.

Anyway, I got through the lunch and it was OK because it was all men. As I mentioned before, most men aren't particularly attuned to "disordered" eating: they don't notice when you accept a bread roll from the basket, wave it around, break it in two, and then leave it on your side plate in a pile of crumbs. They don't see that you lift the olive oil but don't actually drizzle it over your salad at all. Hopefully they didn't find it strange that I asked the waiter three times not to add parmesan to my pasta.

When I eat in public how do I look? I feel like I'm hunched over, tense, the internal conflict in my head plain to see. Could they hear the anorexic voice in my head shouting with each forkful, each fork loaded with fat and calories: greedy, greedy. I don't think they could.

That lunch, day one of my new start: green salad, no dressing, spaghetti with tomato sauce. It wasn't that sinful: quite healthy even. It's indescribable, the taste of real food, when you're used to only apples. Even as I was trying to steer them back to discussing the forthcoming book (they were talking football) my taste buds were being overwhelmed with all the different flavors: fresh egg pasta, drenched, glistening in oil, pesto, and pine nuts muddled with juicy cherry tomatoes, every coiled forkful of spaghetti shining with oil, slick, dripping, fat. My body was so starved of fat that it made me reel.

(I remember when I gave my little niece Isla her first taste of chocolate she looked almost drunk with the new flavor. It was just a nibble on the corner of a chocolate finger, but her eyes lit up and a blissful smile spread across her face. Our bodies are programmed to respond to fat: it's not just me with an insatiable greed, it's not a sin.)

Oh, the relief when that lunch was over. I didn't want to sit in front of the rest of my pasta, because what if I carried on eating? Of course I wouldn't—I had eaten precisely half the plate and laid down my cutlery, but what if I just launched myself into it and finished off every last delicious strand? I always feel like this in restaurants until they collect the plates. As long as the pasta remained there in front of me, I couldn't stop fretting about whether I'd eaten more than half or less than half, and how oily that arrabbiata sauce was. (My lips felt greasy for days from all the oil.)

The ordeal of a simple working lunch: those sleepless nights in advance and ordering unknown food and eating in front of others—do people really enjoy it? It's moments like this that bring me face-to-face with the very real differences in an anorexic brain: I cannot get my head around this concept of enjoying feeding oneself openly, in public. Even now, when Tom glances at his planner, say at breakfast, and realizes he's meeting some PRs for lunch, I marvel at how unplanned he is about going out to eat with strangers. "Saves me a fiver in Pret a Manger" he'll say, and I wonder if I will ever be that relaxed.

When the main course was cleared away I felt a weight lifted from my shoulders. It was perfectly reasonable not to order dessert—I declared myself nicely full and asked for a black filter coffee, decaffeinated. With the horrors of the meal behind me, I felt elated. I sat up straighter, more in control, more professional. I turned to my author and we began to discuss the terms of the contract.

I don't like admitting this stuff, how horribly anorexia got in the way, how it made everything so damn stressful. But I am proud that, despite it all, I did well in my publishing career for more than ten years. You can laugh at my oily-spaghetti horrors (even I am smiling now), but imagine how complicated it made work events, parties, conferences. You're not just having a bite to eat with a colleague or client; you're facing your greatest phobia in public. You're trying to talk business and play the part, and inside there's this shrieking-mad anorexic goading you with every mouthful.

So, was that lovely lunch really a fresh start—my pasta-fueled kick-start to recovery? Not quite. It was a kick-start to nothing, except years more of the same fears. Back at the office, for the rest of the afternoon, my body was silent. It was satiated—a feeling I'm really not accustomed to. I remember there was nothing: no hunger pangs, no cravings. My stomach was peacefully doing its work, I suppose, digesting the nutrients (or whatever full stomachs do with all that fat). The silence unsettled me; there was a dimension missing. There was no edge to anything.

Even cycling home that day was different: I wasn't strung out, so I wasn't flinging myself around corners or weaving through the London traffic. In fact I felt quite patient, and I waited at red lights like I was supposed to. I pedaled along, looking at houses and trees and people walking by. The sun was setting and the evening was mild. I stopped on the bridge in Hyde Park and looked across the Serpentine. There were still a few blue boats out on the water and I almost considered getting off my bike and flopping on the grass with a notebook. There was no reckless rush to get home, I realized—I could just enjoy the evening sunshine. I could stop at a café; I could have a cold beer or a glass of wine al fresco. I could do something spontaneous, unscheduled. But I didn't. It wasn't like me and it felt wrong. When my hunger is stilled there's nothing left to rely on, nothing left inside, and the whole world comes rushing at me. Too many possibilities I can't control. I wanted the hunger back. It focuses me, keeps me on the edge, clean and empty. Fullness, on the other hand, is lazy and contented and complacent. I felt fat and vague and drifting. My body was so quiet.

But this is what I have to accept if I'm going to beat this disease. When I start eating (properly, regularly), yes, I will feel this way. I have to trust that when the hunger goes it will be replaced by something else, something more meaningful than the pain of my stomach acid eating into its lining, the constant thoughts of food. The sensation of fullness, which throws everything off kilter, has to become OK for me somehow. I have to carry on eating, however hard it seems, because I'm running out of excuses and reasons and time.

My spaghetti fears continued way into the night. Twelve hours later I was lying in bed, wide awake, staring into the dark. Finally I turned on the light and sat on the edge of my bed, feeling anxious and defeated. When I got home I'd skipped dinner because of the lunch—that half-plate of pasta—and by midnight of course I was so hungry I couldn't sleep. It was so familiar, the gnawing pain in my gut, the repetitive thoughts. I had to face the fact that I'd failed even before I had made a proper start. And a large part of me was relieved to be sinking back into the welcoming arms of my worst, best friend: hunger.

The reality of getting better is these repeated failures—that's why recovery rates for anorexia are so low. Of course I see it's a pointless waste of time, all these hours spent thinking about what I will and will not eat, what I have and have not eaten. It's cheating and skipping meals and knowing you're only cheating yourself. I find it impossible to silence this internal noise, the commentary on how greedy it is to feed myself. I've always been the energetic one, full-on, slightly manic. Hunger shouldn't give you energy, but paradoxically it does: you're always empty, restless, searching for something to fill you up, always on edge.

So that was another false start. But the point is that I have been here before, many times over the years. According to addiction experts, the more attempts you make to give something up (alcohol, drugs, smoking) the more likely you are to succeed in the end. I have launched myself on this journey of recovery before: I know what it's like to start eating and then lose my nerve and stop. From New York to Oxford to London, in those years from nineteen to twenty-nine, it's no exaggeration to say it's been like that almost every day. I came close to destroying myself and then I began to turn things around; slowly, slowly I began to eat more. And as I began to eat more—falteringly, with plenty of failures along the way—I found that the rest of me came back to life too.

* * *

Back at the start of the millennium, around the time of that lunch, I had begun a relationship with Greg, a man who unfortunately happened to be married with children. He was a Scorpio like I am—completely unstable, but one of the kindest, most intelligent men I'd ever met. We would stay up all night talking over red wine and cigarettes, we argued a lot, shared poetry and music; one evening we just took off and drove for miles, out of London, into the mountains of Snowdonia, and then had to drive all the way back for work. It was like that with Greg: exciting but never relaxing. He was forty-four and I was twenty-four; we were born on the same day exactly twenty years apart. I don't know what I thought was going to happen, if I ever thought about it, though Greg talked of being together forever. By then, I had coaxed myself up to 105 pounds, although it was a constant battle. Anorexia remained my shameful secret, but I was learning to live with it, to work around it. I still wasn't cooking normal meals—or cooking at all—but I was eating: fruit, salad, bread.

As I was starting to find a balance, of sorts, Greg was losing his. In 2002 he killed himself. I still think of him every single day. Ours had been the first relationship in which I'd begun to let my guard down since New York. Sometimes we felt like brother and sister, or father and daughter, or twins; that's how closely entwined we were. I will never know exactly what happened in the final hours before his death, nor what drove him to that ending—I suppose that's why the act of suicide is so hard to accept: there is no explanation, no final goodbye. And of course there are limits on what I can say. Greg had suffered from clinical depression for years and he was experiencing tremendous inner turmoil in those last few months. He was conflicted about his family, his past, our relationship; he was further mixed up by alcohol and the wrong medication, and he was tearing himself apart. Suicide is a cowardly act, but it also takes immense bravery. The philosopher Nietzsche argues that the individual has a full moral right to take his own life, but I'm not so sure. Not when you think about what is left behind. I remember someone once told me: a suicide is tragic because nothing interrupted it . . . Looking back, I understand why Greg took that way out, although it's wrong for anyone to kill oneself in such despair. Why didn't I see what was happening; why didn't I ask someone to help us? I have forgiven him but I will never forgive myself. There is a poem by Emily Brontë called "Remembrance," and it says everything I have ever wanted to say to Greg.

> *Cold in the earth—and the deep snow piled above thee,*
> *Far, far removed, cold in the dreary grave!*
> *Have I forgot, my only Love, to love thee,*
> *Severed at last by Time's all-severing wave?*

I remember the phone call at dawn telling me his body had been found that beautiful day in September. The leaves were turning red and gold and there was the first hint of coolness in the air. Then the postmortem, and the following weekend my big sister's wedding, and Greg's funeral, which I was not allowed to attend. Weeks later, the local vicar secretly agreed to take me to where he had been buried. Sitting beside his freshly dug grave was one of the bleakest moments of my life: it didn't seem possible that his body was really lying there, a few feet below me.

Then weeks, months of unremitting hell inside my head, where the questions and guilt and grief and love collided without solace or answers. I never got to say goodbye. I never got to hold him one last time.

Now, my parents tell me they were convinced Greg's death would send me back down into full-on anorexia. It sort of did, and sort of didn't. I lost a lot of weight at the time—the pink silk bridesmaid dress for my sister's wedding had to be taken in and in and in as the pounds dropped off. Katie's wedding photographs show me pale and paper-thin. But I don't remember consciously avoiding food, so I don't think this was anorexia—just a complete absence of appetite through grief. Even now, I can't think clearly about that time without feeling panicky. The grieving process for Greg was like an extended panic attack that lasted months— bewildering, relentless.

For a long time afterward I wanted to die too. Greg had loved me fiercely for two years (I sometimes found his love claustrophobic), but more than that he had protected me. Previous boyfriends had been around the same age as I, but Greg was twenty years older. He was at a different stage in life; he was powerful, he made me feel safe. Without him I felt frightened and alone. I did not think I could carry on living. But his suicide taught me something I have clung to ever since: that I could not destroy my family in that way. I would not leave behind me the mess he left behind. My father's parents committed suicide and he has never recovered. Although I love Greg with all my heart, although I understand he had no other option, although I know he was brave, still I believe suicide is a profoundly selfish act. Whatever happens I will not take that way out. Suicide is not an option.

I think this belief—that you must go on living, whatever happens—saved me. After almost a year of hovering in between, I got back on track. By the first anniversary of Greg's death, I was starting to look around me again, starting to see that life could be worth a try. With that new hope came a little bit of weight and then a bit more. I've maintained a fragile equilibrium ever since, between 98 and 112 pounds. And that's about where we are now. Early April, springtime, Greg's favorite season.

Did I waste those years? Do I regret it all? Please . . . I can barely bring myself to answer. I want to believe that nothing is wasted. Life, even after suicide, even with anorexia, is still worth living. There was happiness and sadness, lots of work and relationships and books and therapy, there was a year of raw grief I have tried to block out. If I could go back, of course there are things I would change: I would have seen what was happening with Greg, I would have sought help. But I was only twenty-four. And there is no way of going back. He left a wife and children, and their loss is so much greater than mine.

* * *

While we're on endings, there is a postscript to the Laurie story too. Nine years after we broke up, when I was twenty-eight, we met in London. His mother was lecturing in town and our two families went out for dinner, a pleasant Italian meal. I ate garlic bread, salad, and pasta like the others—I desperately wanted to appear normal—although unlike the others I had saved up my calories for this event for days.

After the meal, Laurie and I stayed on at the restaurant in Bloomsbury. We had a few more glasses of wine in the bar, then sat talking in Russell Square all night, then we walked down to the Thames and watched the sun rise before I had to go to the office. It was as wonderful as I had known it would be, walking and talking with Laurie; all the old magic was back.

Following that brief encounter, he invited me to New York for a long weekend. That too was bittersweet: perfect and yet heartbreaking at the same time. We went to the New York City Ballet, met up with old friends for brunch, took long, nostalgic strolls around Central Park, drank red wine at Blue Note, our favorite jazz club. For me it was magical being back in Manhattan, being with Laurie again: I liked us even more in our late twenties than as teenagers. But it became clear that he saw this as a couple of days of fun together, nothing more. Certainly he had no long-term plans for a future that included me. I flew back from New York on the Monday morning with my heart in pieces—it sounds crazy, but I felt I was holding the raw chunks of it in my hands.

That week I returned to London, I lost 8, 9, 10 pounds—my body just went into weight-loss free fall.

I only mention this because it seems incredible that, after nine years, he had not lost the power to hurt. Leaving him that last time, knowing he would never love me the way I loved him, the anorexia rushed back in like an old habit. I remember lying on the wooden floor of my Elephant & Castle flat, talking to my mother on the phone, and crying so hard the tears running off my face pooled on the bare floorboards around me. That was the end, I knew it then at last, and I have not seen him since.

That was more than six years ago; Laurie is now married and has two daughters. From that final meeting, it would be more than four years before I would meet Tom, and at least five years until I even felt ready to contemplate recovery.

* * *

I find it overwhelming, at times, trying to understand the past. My twenties were a difficult decade, no doubt about that. Mostly it was the slow, daily fight against the voice inside my head that tells me (always) I'm greedy and I don't deserve to eat. The voice that reminds me I'll get fat the moment I let my guard down. Compared to rowing across the Indian Ocean, say, or overcoming cancer, the food struggles are nothing—an extra yogurt or an additional piece of toast. But it's the relentless voice inside that makes anorexia such a fight.

And now, if I want to have a baby, I have to make the last colossal push: I have to get out of the underweight hinterland, this just not-well zone; I have to drag myself back into the world of breasts and periods and flesh and being a woman. I've done it before; surely I can do it again? Faced with the same challenge, I try to recall what worked last time. All I remember is the pain of each cheese sandwich. (Yes, cheese!)

What is holding me back? I could be so close to a breakthrough. They say that when you're overweight it's losing the last few pounds that is most difficult. I think it's the same with gaining them.

* * *

Sometimes it's frightening, writing this book. I lie awake most nights and think about the ending. You know how it's supposed to end, right?

As I write, I'm still trying, every day, to make myself eat more and not panic and not give up. It's April now, nearly six months since I embarked on this journey. I have put on weight and it's exciting and threatening. I must be 108, maybe 112 pounds—I'm not sure, I can't face weighing myself. But it's the furthest I've ever gotten and it's a huge psychological barrier for me. I feel large, and my clothes feel tight; at night I feel overheated. But this is progress: this is exactly what has to happen. I cycle all over London and I feel powerful—I have more energy—I can see my body is starting to respond.

I could be very close to a breakthrough, Tom reminds me; I could be closer than I think. I know he's right: I have to be strong and not retreat . . . At times the fear is so great—of changing, of fat, of losing control. I find myself physically clenching my teeth, my fists; I have to hold my nerve. If I retreat now, what was it all for?

I swing from optimism to panic: some days I'm excited and some days I'm in despair. I am tense, waiting—like a bomb is about to go off. I know I have to put on this weight but I dread it. I know this is a normal part of recovery: the ups and downs are inevitable. Last week, for example, the sun came out and everyone started talking about how winter was finally at an end. So I decided it was time for a spring-clean, and I spent the evening going through boxes of documents, bank statements, letters. I found a file of medical referrals from the last ten years, mostly from my psychiatrist Dr. Robinson to my GP. It made depressing reading. "Emma has reached a BMI of 17 but remains amenorrheic"; "She has lost 3 lbs but appears to want to recover"; "Her bone scan shows further deterioration, results attached."

Suddenly it was like a needle had punctured my spring optimism. For the first time I felt defeated; I thought, *I can't do this*. The evidence was spread out in front of me in black and white: all the doctors' reports, the consultations and weigh-ins, my inability to reach a healthy BMI; charts with zigzags showing the ups and downs, tiny losses and tiny gains (which felt so huge at the time), two pounds higher then six pounds lower, one step forward and two steps back.

I thought of all the effort I put in, all the time I'd wasted. No one will ever understand, and what does it matter? Year after year of not eating and I've got nothing to show for it but this hopeless bunch of doctors' letters. I've given the last decade to anorexia and gotten nowhere. Sitting there on the living room floor, feeling hopeless, I recalled a warning from a psychotherapist about recognizing one's own limitations: "If it was simply a matter of reason and persistence you'd probably have recovered by now. It may not just be about willpower."

I really was defeated. At that moment, I felt, *I've been kidding myself*. I thought I was well on the way to beating this—I thought this was finally my new start. Maybe the reason I haven't gotten better is that I can't. It's not about food or weight. There's a reason why anorexics don't ever recover fully. I'll never be free of this, no matter how hard I try.

I abandoned the spring-cleaning and retreated to a hot bath, shaken by this epiphany. If I can't beat this illness, then what next? I like to know where I'm going but at that moment I was rudderless. Sinking under the grapefruit-scented bubbles I wondered: *Is acceptance the most mature thing?* People live with other challenging conditions: schizophrenia, bipolar disorder, depression. Perhaps I need to learn to live with anorexia and make peace with myself. After all, it's not anorexia itself that torments me; it's constantly struggling against it. Surely it's possible to be happy, however imperfectly?

But then, what about having a family with Tom? I want our baby so much. My mind was racing, unable to admit defeat. I needed a plan. I got out of the bath, wrapped myself in a towel, and opened my laptop. I Googled "fertility drugs, IVF, adoption."

Later that evening I wrote my weekly column, and I decided to be completely honest. I explained my despair, I admitted I had failed so many times before and now I feared I would probably fail again. The responses started coming in within hours of publication:

April 20, 2011 5:58 PM
Hi Emma—OK so you have had a little relapse. It doesn't mean you can't do this. You are not anorexic—you just have this negative voice that pervades your life called anorexia. You can take charge of your life—you can change it. There are many young women like you who have managed to have a child—it has been life-changing for them and so worthwhile. So just shake this negative voice out of your head and carry on—it is a privilege to share your journey—you are so brave and honest—maybe get some CBT or hypnotherapy—anything to get you back on track—YOU CAN DO THIS!!
J.M.
April 20, 2011 8:22 PM

Wishing you all the very best in your personal comeback. I spent most of my forties and my early fifties firstly driven by and then fighting against my anorexia. I'm fifty-seven now, and while I do still get anorexic thoughts, I'm able to eat, drink AND LIVE in spite of them. A massive motivation has been my grandson who's 20 months old now. I wanted to be well, to be able to help my daughter, to enjoy my grandson and to enjoy grandmotherhood— and to be me. Take care, Emma, Be gentle with yourself—and be proud of yourself.
V.B.

April 21, 2011 11:51 AM
You absolutely cannot give up now. Anorexia may always be with you mentally but that doesn't mean you can't keep up all your hard work and gain weight physically. Don't think you'll not be able to overcome anorexia this time round just because you've failed in the past, you're making great progress and you will be able to naturally conceive your own child naturally, not just take the easy way out and opt for IVF, etc. We're all behind you on this.
C.J.

* * *

Just as I was close to throwing in the towel, something shifted and my mood lifted. The sunshine helped, and the readers' responses helped, and I was back in the ring . . . I've noticed that life is often this way: when we're about to give up, something happens. Yes, I felt beaten, and yes, I'd started investigating fertility drugs. (Despite what the reader said, that isn't the "easy way out"; in fact going through IVF or other forms of assisted conception can be much more emotionally and physically demanding than natural conception.) But I'd also received some fantastic support, reminding me there's plenty of fight left in me. My Canadian friend Mike had emailed:

You don't need to think about IVF, not yet—this sounds like a cop-out to me. The truth is there was a time in your life when you were not anorexic; you have to return to that state. That beautiful baby needs to come from you, it needs your genes, you owe it to yourself.

From Switzerland, my friend Sunray emailed to say:

Your feelings at the moment aren't weird, they're normal! But you have to find a way to succeed, scary or not, because the problem won't go away until you do. You want a family—that has to be your weapon. Use it to make you stubborn. Your future baby needs you to fight the fears . . .

At *Times Online*, a woman wrote:

I'm at the opposite end of the weight spectrum, trying not to eat cake (amongst other things) so it scares both of us for pretty much the same reason: one bite and I know I'll lose control. Don't worry about IVF for now, just keep thinking of the baby, and keep eating.

I was seriously considering the fertility drug Clomiphene—my thinking was, *Well, if slim actresses and models can pop it like Smarties, why shouldn't I?* If I honestly can't gain the weight required to get pregnant, and I'm not getting any younger, surely there must be another way? Fortunately, my GP said no. He reminded me that the proper use of fertility drugs was to treat infertility, and said, "You're not infertile, you're underweight."

And he's right. I can't keep avoiding the weight issue. I suppose that Clomiphene might get me pregnant by stimulating ovulation, but who knows if my body would be able to keep the baby?

And then I got an email from my former psychiatrist, Dr. Robinson.

The recovery process has been likened to getting an Oscar. You don't know if you'll make it until your name is called, then all your anxiety erupts into stage fright and your emotions don't settle down for ages. I say, keep going until your ovary system signals that your body is healthy enough to carry and feed a child.

Needless to say, my column the following week was much more optimistic. It was written while I was sitting on my balcony in spring sunshine, and I can still recall the sense of adventure, the elation packed into every word.

I want to tell you how this feels, these past few months: it's been like a rebirth. My body is waking up. Everything is a new experience: tastes, sensations, emotions. And I'm appalled at my honesty. For my entire adult life I've been pretending I'm fine (I'm not hungry, no really, I just ate) but now I've come out and everyone can see that I'm not fine at all. I've done something I never, ever do: I've asked for help. To everyone who writes and believes I can do it: I read all your messages and I want to burst with joy because I think you might be right.

Chapter 7
Confessions of a Travel Writer's Girlfriend

"Wow, what an amazing job." This (after "So what *do* you eat?") is the comment I hear most often. And yes, Tom's job is amazing—he's a travel writer and hotel reviewer for a national newspaper, so we get to travel the world, exploring fantastic islands and beaches and cities. When we're in the U.K. we spend almost every weekend out of London, traveling to review yet another hip hotel for his weekly column.

Tom and I thrive on perpetual motion. We talk and explore and hatch plans for the future: our books, our columns, our trips, our baby. While he reviews the hotels, I've become the unofficial spa sidekick, submitting (willingly) to beauty treatments and reporting back. This involves facials and body wraps, manicures and pedicures, eyebrow threading and hot stone therapy and massages galore. I've become something of a spa expert, which is pretty funny for the scholarship girl from St. Paul's who could never afford to get blonde streaks in her hair. My latest discovery is eyelash tinting: they paint something onto your eyes and it's like permanent mascara without the risk of smudging or the hassle of makeup remover.

There's no doubt that Tom has a dream job as a travel writer and journalist—although we sometimes long to spend a weekend at home in London, not driving or chatting to hotel managers, or packing and unpacking our bags. Strictly speaking, I'm a journalist too now, with my weekly column—but as usual I feel like a fraud. I suppose I'm still in the uncertain phase of not really knowing how to describe myself or what it is I do, a phase familiar to all those who have stepped out of the daily office environment. It's been more than nine months since I left my full-time job in publishing but, after ten years working in large companies, that dinner-party question, "So what do *you* do?" still makes me hesitate. Just last month, as the April tax deadline approached, I had to fill in an Inland Revenue self-assessment form, and my pen wavered when I reached the "occupation" box.

Leaving full-time employment has been a considerable challenge, both in financial and lifestyle terms; at times I've found it as testing as my simultaneous quest to beat anorexia. We don't realize, I think, how much our professional roles define us, and how much of our self-esteem is tied up with being part of an organization, of a gang, with feeling "useful." But overall it's been a liberating move and one I don't regret: I felt that a decade working for various corporations had earned me the chance to try something different, to pursue the writing career I'd always dreamed of. Within a month of going freelance I had a literary agent, and within six months I'd finished my first novel. Getting a regular column in *The Times* was just the icing on the cake.

And the travel works well for both of us: as writers, Tom and I just need our laptops. I don't bother to put my suitcase away anymore—when we get back from a trip I leave it in the spare room—and I carry my passport with me all the time. I will often wake up, in an unfamiliar room in an unfamiliar bed, and not know where I am. As a green semi-vegan who cycles everywhere, recycles everything, doesn't drive, and rarely turns on the central heating, I know this relationship isn't environmentally friendly. In our defense, we always travel to Europe by train, and we offset our flights. In addition to the carbon footprint, I detest flying; if it were possible, I'd never board another plane ever again.

A woman I know, an obstetrician at St. Thomas's Hospital in London, recently told me that if I wanted to have a baby, I should slow down. "You need to relax in order to conceive. Stop traveling, stop cycling, stop staying up all night writing." I understand this in principle, but I don't know how to put it into practice: slowing down would mean a total change of lifestyle.

When it comes to other people's journalism, because of our own experiences I like to read between the lines: I'm always curious when A.A. Gill, the restaurant critic, refers to his partner as "the blonde." *Does she like eating out all the time?* I wonder. *Does she get to choose the restaurant?* Have you ever wondered, reading travel pieces in a magazine, what the journalist's other half is up to?

Lots of jet lag for starters (and the odd jet-lagged fight). And airports and rental cars and spa treatments and wine bars and hotels and sunburns and tourist offices. (Tom has an obsession with tourist information centers. If we see one, wherever we are, he has to go in and collect every single flyer and brochure available.) And lots of churches and beaches, art galleries and museums.

And, in my case, lots of food dodging. Turns out it's not easy having an eating disorder when you're a travel writer's girlfriend.

* * *

There are so many ways not to eat. There is straightforward food-avoidance: "I'm not hungry" or "I'll have something later." Then there's the more refined kind, at which I excel, whereby anything is used as a reason not to eat.

This morning, in a hotel in Edinburgh, I left the breakfast table without eating because the orange on my plate was full of seeds and slightly sour and it had too much white pith and was impossible to peel . . . and the apples were Granny Smiths, and they'd presliced them when I prefer them whole, and the bananas were too green. And so on and so on (while Tom calmly ate his porridge and toast with strawberry jam). I don't know why I couldn't eat something else, but the orange was a disaster and the voice inside (guilt and anxiety) shouts at me, and it all becomes impossible. Something flips in my brain—it's chemical I think; I'm not in control. I've been told that eating might actually help to calm these feelings but I don't know about that.

According to Tom I said, "I can't eat now, I'm too stressed from that orange. Forget it, I'll just have coffee."

Too *stressed* from an orange? Just another excuse for dodging. Recently I've been having issues with cutlery. If a fork is too large, I can't use it. When we're on the road, I can't eat with a plastic spoon—I mostly carry a small spoon in my handbag but sometimes we forget. (I notice I'm developing a thing about spoons: I have a drawer at home and I've just counted nineteen perfect silver spoons in there.) Plates need to be right as well—I don't mind small plates, but I cannot eat on a large dinner plate. Also temperatures: I can't eat food that's too hot, but if it's gone stone-cold, forget that too. Same with mouth-feel: too hard isn't good (bread) and too soft is hopeless, especially when it comes to pasta. My father is the king of spaghetti, and he always cooks it perfectly *al dente*: he doesn't even need to test it—he can "hear" when pasta is ready just from the sound of the bubbling water in the pan.

The consistency of fruit is also crucial for me: hard green bananas are no good, but overripe (over-sugary) ones are also inedible. Same with apples: bruised or pulpy is impossible. Grapes must be shiny and firm, no seeds. Then there's sweet with savory—raisins crop up everywhere, and I find any dried fruit with savory off-putting. I don't understand why Marks & Spencer have started adding pomegranates to their otherwise perfect Super Wholefood Couscous, and I have to weed out every single one. When I look at food that is "wrong" I just think, *Well, I won't bother. Forget it.* Baked beans need to be eaten cold from the fridge, with a small spoon, and preferably in a small can.

I'm being flippant, but it's less amusing in practice. In essence, I can't eat normal food like a normal person: this is what anorexia means. To me, these rules make total sense, but they're just another way of avoiding food. It's incredibly stressful for Tom, I know, and of course it stops me from recovering. "I know exactly what you like, Em," he tells me. "It has to be pure and fresh and totally untouched. I can see from a glance at a breakfast buffet whether we're going to have a problem." He's right. My food has to be a certain way—and when you travel as much as we do, it rarely is.

* * *

I sound really fussy, I know. But these are the rules that govern me. I wouldn't call it fussy eating; it goes way beyond that. Faced with unfamiliar food that isn't the way I can eat it: I'm not being childish; I simply can't eat it. The sense of impotence when food isn't "right," when you're starving, is hard to convey . . . Most people get touchy when they're hungry, right? Imagine that hunger and irritability, but magnified, when you really haven't eaten for hours, when there is nothing you can eat. I can only describe it as food rage.

Tom and I have had scenes and food missions and mishaps all over the world. Back in November, not long after I started writing the column, we visited Tanzania:

I'm gripping the edges of the table really hard, willing myself not to freak out. The urge to hurl the plate of food across the restaurant is overwhelming, to overturn the table, to kick over chairs. Instead I stand up, taking care not to trip on my maxi dress, and walk out, leaving T and the waiters staring after me.

What's happening to me? I admit I've always been fiery but these sudden flashes of anger, this food rage, is completely new. Is this just about relinquishing anorexia? It's like I'm transferring the rigid control I used to have over food somewhere else. Is that too simplistic? Maybe my emotions are out of control because I'm out of control. Whatever the reason, my moods are all over the place and I don't know who I am or what to do. I'm angry and frightened.

So began our first evening in Africa.

It wasn't such a big deal I suppose, but imagine you're jet-lagged, starving hungry, and craving something nutritious; you order steamed vegetables and rice and you check repeatedly that they understand what this means—"Steamed not fried, please"—and then they bring you carrots and rice drenched in butter with a side order of fried sweet potato.

How could I eat food that was swimming in butter? I couldn't, is the simple answer. I didn't ask for anything special; I wanted them simply not to mess with my food. Is this an example of anorexic thinking; is this overly controlling, unreasonable?

For me, it always comes back to this issue of control. I turned to anorexia late on—until the age of nineteen, food and I were fine. Not eating was a way of punishing myself for being inadequate, for getting dumped; unfortunately anorexia offers surprisingly swift rewards. You starve, you get thin; you have control. Yes, finally you have control over something! Of course, when you're seriously thin you're not in control at all. By the final year of university I'd lost nearly half my body weight. At that level there's nothing rational left: the brain is a muscle, and it wastes away just like the rest of your muscles. I would walk around Oxford at 3 AM, 4 AM alone, freezing, smoking.

But anorexia has been my way of controlling the uncontrollable world out there, a way of keeping other people out. It's me saying, "I don't need your love, I don't trust your food, I don't want to join in." It's a rejection of the outside world. Truthfully, I never meant to isolate myself—I used to be the life and soul of the party . . . but when you've been badly hurt, it's safer to be alone.

Now, when Tom tries to look after me and I reject that, of course it's all about control, isn't it? When he asks me, yet again, to move in with him, instead of feeling loved I feel threatened. At the most basic level food is about nurture and care, and I don't always seem to be able to accept that or trust in it. When I do relax and allow Tom to look after me—whether that's running a hot bubble bath or bringing me breakfast in bed—it's a wonderful, peaceful feeling, like being a child, safe again.

Tom wants me to beat anorexia because he loves me, not because I'm weak. Why can't I accept that? Why is letting someone else in so hard—why does it feel like such a loss of control? And why, when they mess up my food, why can't I just eat it anyway?

In Tanzania I lived on pineapple. For an entire week. When we got back, my mouth and tongue were so ulcerated I could barely speak.

In Tanzania, Kenya, and other countries we've been to in Africa, most dishes are prepared in oil, butter, or ghee. That's just the way they cook; it's a cultural thing, and it can be hard to get them to do it any other way. We've been treated to top chefs and private dining, butlers in villas and romantic barbecues on the beach, star-lit meals on dhows and candle-lit dinners on our veranda. Vegetables (my food of choice) are never a problem in Africa; they have delicious carrots, broccoli, and beans in abundance. But somewhere between the kitchen and the dinner table, it all goes horribly wrong. I have lost count of the number of evenings when, after requesting a plate of steamed vegetables—sometimes even writing down the request with clear, polite instructions: *Please just steam, please do not fry or add butter*—the vegetables have arrived at the table swimming in oil.

Carrots in butter? Broccoli glistening with oil? I can't do it.

I know what you're thinking: what a waste. What a miserable, controlling woman; what an unadventurous way to travel. You're right, and my boyfriend would probably agree with you. When he tried fruit-bat curry in the Seychelles (and I ate a plain green salad) I remember feeling sad that I couldn't join in. Obviously, one of the best things about foreign travel is foreign cuisine. But there is nothing more frightening to an anorexic than unknown food.

* * *

Driving through the Italian Alps a few weeks ago, on our way to a ski trip, we were remembering some of last year's adventures. We reminisced about the baboons in Kenya (the hotel was overrun with them and they stole my bananas) and how we drove all over Barbados looking for low-fat yogurt. We'd finally found some imported Müllers in a supermarket in Bridgetown and bought the whole stock! I ate them even though I suspected they might not be low-fat (they tasted suspiciously full-fat); that's how desperate I was.

Tom was remembering the problems we had in Zanzibar over bread rolls. We'd just arrived on the Spice Islands on a tiny six-seater propeller plane from Dar es Salaam, and we were cooling off in the plunge pool and trying to order dinner. It was nearly 100 degrees that first night and there was nothing I could eat on the room service menu. Tom was desperate to find something so he went to talk to the chef, to see if they could whip up some basic hummus or tzatziki (natural yogurt with cucumber) and maybe some bread rolls. These foods are on my "safe" list (although I hate the uncertainty of foreign versions: how exactly have they prepared them?).

Poor Tom, dripping with sweat and travel-weary, standing in that kitchen, trying to explain to the Tanzanian cooks how to make bread. They're not big on brown bread in Zanzibar, apparently, so the whole concept was alien to them. We thought: *water, flour, mold it into lumps*—is that even right? Who knows how you make bread?—and sort of knead it around and then bake it in the oven. He finally staggered back to the villa with a silver tray of tiny, burned, button-lumps of flour, and we both dissolved into hysterics. It was beyond a joke (and I was really hungry!) but he said they looked like "pregnant Maltesers" and it released all the tension.

I won't go into the episode when we tried to make yogurt in a hotel kitchen in Kenya. I don't actually know how you make yogurt (or bread, clearly). It's all to do with yeast and fermentation and leaving things to set, or rise, or something. Anyway, Tom and I didn't have a clue about the quantities or technique involved, and the results were disastrous: three large ramekins of soured, full-fat milk brought to our table every morning. Not yogurt. It was warm, like it had just come out of a cow, and curdled. (God, how I longed for Marks & Spencer.)

I'm starting to realize that I missed out on learning to cook. When other people were experimenting with recipes and holding elaborate dinner parties at university, I was starving myself.

Food has never been that kind of adventure for me, and I've never bought a cookbook, unless *The Food Doctor Diet* counts. Looking at my bookshelves now, I see I've been given a couple of cookbooks over the years—*Simple Vegetarian Cooking, Healthy Indian Food*—but I've never opened them. Many anorexics spend hours in the kitchen preparing elaborate meals for others, but I don't want to be around food. I flick straight past the food sections in the Sunday magazines (looking at those complicated food photographs repulses me).

I'm just not interested in cooking. I'm more comfortable with pure, cold food than hot meals. I prefer muesli with fresh organic milk, or a can of baked beans from the fridge. I had a new kitchen installed in my flat three years ago when I moved in. The previous tenants had defaulted on their mortgage, which is why I was able to afford a flat in Islington, and as part of their revenge shenanigans they ripped out the fitted kitchen and ran off with it. So I had this lovely silver and black chrome kitchen installed, but I've never even taken the instruction manual out of the oven.

* * *

One of the responses to my column that hurt me most (early on, before I toughened up) was, "If you can't feed yourself, how are you ever going to feed a baby?" In other words, sort out your own attitude to food and eating before you try to bring up a child. Is this right? And if I'm a bad cook, does that stop me from being a good mother? If I have anorexia, does that mean I can't look after my baby?

Who knows what makes good parents; who knows when anyone is ever "ready" for a child? Tom and I have talked about this a lot recently: he is about to turn forty. For him, the desire to become a father has been quite sudden. It may be that women are biologically programmed to get broody: we have responsibility from early on for conception and contraception, so we tend to think about it and discuss it more than men. Even if you're not feeling particularly broody, as a woman it's hard to escape the dire warnings about plummeting fertility. But perhaps this business of being "ready" is just a red herring: I've watched my brothers and sisters, friends and colleagues, younger and older, many of whom aren't exactly parent material, and they get through it, they have their babies and they love them; it all works out in the end.

I don't think any couple can ever be 100 percent ready. Of course Tom and I aren't totally prepared for parenthood; that's the whole point, it's a journey into the unknown. But I don't think this is just me being broody—or Tom playing along to make me happy. I can see it in his eyes and I believe him when he tells me how much he wants us to have a child. And we agree that we're as ready as we're ever going to be.

(I know I'm jumping ahead of myself here. I'm not even pregnant, this is the whole point, and I'm not going to get pregnant unless I can gain enough weight.)

* * *

But then . . . what about all this travel? Is having a baby really compatible with this peripatetic lifestyle, footloose and fancy-free, a different hotel every weekend, a new country every couple of weeks? My eating disorder isn't the only thing under threat here: I think we need to accept that having a baby will force us to slow down. Babies need stability and routine—hell, *I* need stability and routine—and it might not be possible to go on passport-stamp collecting at such a rate.

In the past, our attempts to slow down have had limited success. We come back from a big trip—say, two weeks in South Africa last

Christmas, just before I ate that memorable Kit Kat—and we say we'll take a break from traveling, spend more time at home, enjoy London and catch up with friends. It never lasts. I remember after Cape Town we didn't book any trips or hotels for a few weeks, resolutely staying home. Then I caught Tom lingering over the travel section in *The Sunday Telegraph*, we both started tearing out new hotel features, and before long we were packing to go skiing in a remote corner of the Bernese Oberland. Itchy feet . . .

A few days ago I heard a neuroscientist and psychologist on Radio 4 discussing a possible link between autism and anorexia. At first, this seemed tenuous, but as I listened I became intrigued. Could there be something in this new research, something to do with the inability to relate (characteristic of the autism spectrum) and the dissociative state of anorexia, the denial of hunger, the detachment from the body? The research is still at an early stage, but it doesn't seem so far-fetched: for some reason I feel utterly detached from my body, and I respond to hunger differently from other people. As I've tried to show, this is more than just a diet gone wrong: I watch others eating and I have a strong sense that my brain is wired differently.

And then it made me think about travel, and why Tom and I are always moving. What is the travel really about? Of course there's the excitement of seeing new places and learning about the world; it's a great privilege and an adventure. It inspires us both, and it opens one's eyes to different people, languages, and cultures. But it's also a great way to avoid facing up to problems within oneself.

Perpetual motion seems to calm me—I can't sit still for long; jogging and cycling and swimming help me cope with the clamor in my head. At night, I rub my feet gently against each other, rub, rub, rub, hour after hour, to soothe myself; I curl my hands up tight under my chin to make me feel safe in bed (Tom calls it tucking) and shift them about throughout the night, trying to get secure.

My mother has a photograph of me, taken a few hours after my birth at the Hammersmith and West London Hospital: my hand is curled into a tiny fist and tucked under my chin—apparently I've always done that. As a child I used to rock myself to sleep (another feature of autism), and even now I find rhythmical rocking quite reassuring.

I wonder if perhaps this need for speed, this perpetual wanderlust, is a mild addiction. Or is something worrying me so much that I can't stay still?

Then again, I also enjoy coming home: after weeks on the road, long-haul flights and unfamiliar settings, staying alert, living out of a bag, being at the mercy of airline crews or hotel staff—finally the familiarity of one's own space. I enjoy unlocking the front door (and feeling the relief of not having been burgled), hauling my suitcase upstairs, sorting through the mail, chucking out the pizza flyers and the *Hackney Gazette*, loading the laundry into the washing machine, taking a shower, and lying down, clean and exhausted. My own bed. Home at last. The homecoming is all part of traveling.

So when that obstetrician advises me to slow down, stay home, rest up, I know it's not going to happen. Tom and I are travelers. Our baby will have to come along too.

Chapter 8
Miracle Cures

D   *ear Emma, I have been following your columns with interest.
    I am a clinical hypnotherapist working with clients on "mind
over matter" challenges. I wonder if you might be interested in a
free session of hypnotherapy to support you? I think this could
provide a safe environment for you to experience some powerful
transitions . . .*

Powerful transitions, eh? Another day, another email out of
the blue offering help. After all these years of keeping things
locked up inside, I'm amazed how much support there is if you
ask for it.

As I mentioned, my obstetrician friend says that slowing down
could be the key to recovery. My mindfulness guru tells me I
need to stop saying sorry and to stop feeling guilty. My mother
says I need more cheese, healthy fats, and oils in my diet, and my
boyfriend says I should move in with him. A woman from Paris
emails that I should start eating meat and fish again, a professional
cyclist from Scotland writes that "seven pots of cottage cheese per
week" has been the key to his physical rehabilitation. My little
sister tells me about EFT, the emotional freedom technique, my
aunt about EMDR, an eye movement desensitization therapy.
Some people swear by meditation, yoga, or Ayurveda, others

have recommended nutritional supplements. I attend a six-week insomnia course, I have weekly acupuncture sessions and visit a homeopathic doctor, I try to do my morning visualizations, I skim-read *The Power of Now*, I plough through a 600-page tome called *Miraculous Healings*, I look into Neuro-Linguistic Programming.

All these miracle cures and still I find the hardest thing is eating. Over the years I've tried all these things and many more . . . and, as I've said, I don't think there is a silver bullet. If you've ever tried giving up smoking you may have experienced this kind of support overload and still found yourself reaching for a cigarette at the end of it. The truth is, all the hypnosis and Allen Carr books and nicotine gum won't help you quit if you still *want* to smoke. I smoked from the age of sixteen to twenty-nine, and I never thought I'd be able to kick it. The simple fact was, I loved it. I've heard it said we're born as smokers or as nonsmokers: my big sister, Katie, for example, is rabidly antismoking, and it's impossible to imagine her with a cigarette in her hands, whereas my other sisters and brothers are all either smokers or ex-smokers. And my parents too: Dad is a reformed ex-smoker but in his heyday he smoked cigarettes, cigars, pipes, cheroots, and took snuff. He gave up forty years ago but he admits he still sometimes misses an after-dinner smoke with a glass of brandy. My mum, on the other hand, just like Katie, has never even tried a cigarette.

For me, the turning point with smoking came when I began actively to dislike it. I was sick of stinking like an ashtray and being a social outcast and having to stand in the freezing cold outside the office puffing away with other losers and the rising price of cigarettes and developing a disgusting cough and wheezing in the mornings. It took thirteen years to get there, and I was still hooked on the nicotine (a substance more addictive than heroin), but I had to start really hating smoking and wanting to be an ex-smoker before I could attempt to give it up.

It's the same with an eating disorder—you have to get sick of it before you're ready to give it up. For all the support and advice in the world, I'm starting to believe that the single most important component to recovery is wanting it, really, really wanting to be free of anorexia.

It's the end of April and I've been writing the column in *The Times* for nearly six months now. During that time many girls have emailed me asking for advice—as if I'm in a position to help! I can see their logic, but it seems a bit like consulting a drug addict in rehab (especially when I've had a really bad day, and I've dodged my morning banana and halved my lunchtime apple, and then I get an email asking me how to put on weight). I'm not sure whether they actually want advice—when you're twenty-one and burning up your own body fat and muscle, when you're young and thin and beautiful, you feel untouchable—but I'd love to stop them from going through what I went through. Often, it's clear they just need to tell someone the worst things: the way they vomit after every meal, how their throats are bleeding, the massive laxative abuse (100 tablets a day), the self-harm and the razors.

And, once in a while, a death. Yesterday I received this email:

Dear Emma,

Having followed your articles in The Times *for the past few months, I would like to pass on my best wishes in your fight against anorexia. I have admired your gutsy spirit and determination, and hope you can manage to get on top of this dreadful illness. I'm sure there are many low, as well as high, points but your reporting so far sounds very positive.*

My daughter suffered from anorexia for ten years, like yourself, but found the constant battles just too difficult, and disappeared while on leave from hospital just a couple of months ago. She was found, six weeks later, in the river close to our home, where she had originally driven the car on the night she went missing. Our grief is still overwhelming and we wish she could have got to the stage where she had the strength to fight this illness. But at least we know she is at last at peace.

Our very best wishes go out to you, I dearly hope this illness can be beaten and that you realize your wonderful ambition of becoming a mother.
Regards,
Mrs. V

It was a sunny Tuesday morning, unseasonably hot for late April; I had the balcony doors open and was sitting at my breakfast bar, typing away at my laptop, barefoot, in denim shorts and a bright blue Inca Cola T-shirt Tom had brought back from Mexico, when the red light on my Blackberry started flashing. I picked it up, read the quoted message above, put it down and carried on working. A few minutes later I stopped, and reread the message, and called home. I needed to speak to my mum.

I try to reply to every email, especially those asking for advice, but I don't know if it makes any difference. And when I look back, I wonder if anything would have made me give up anorexia in my twenties: I was high on hunger; I felt untouchable too. For all my attempts to get better, did I really want it enough? What I always want to say to these girls with anorexia, bulimia, and worse, but in a more eloquent form, is: *Stop now . . . give it up right now and don't waste the years ahead, and don't kid yourself that there's some point to being hungry or that it gives you any control over things because it doesn't and life is uncontrollable and anorexia is just another way of hiding . . .*

A wise man once said: never take the advice of someone who has not had your kind of trouble.

Which is why, even though I have anorexia, I strangely *do* feel qualified to offer advice. In a funny way I'm more expert than a doctor or specialist, because I've been through recovery and I'm still going through it. I got myself from 77 to 105 pounds, bite by agonizing bite, and there's still more work to do. I don't have the secret to an instant, perfect recovery—and it's impossible to generalize when everyone is different—but I am intimately familiar with the dangers and triggers. If nothing else, I understand what helps and what harms . . .

My number one tip for recovery is this: get rid of your thin clothes. Go through your wardrobe and chuck out the size zeros. Be ruthless; do it now. Sounds trivial but it's crucial: so much of how you feel about eating and food and yourself, walking around in daily life, is inside your head. Anyone would be uncomfortable in tight clothing, and anorexics are particularly susceptible to this kind of body panic. I know it's tough: taking my J Brand skinny jeans to the thrift shop was hell. But really, why are you wearing age-fourteen clothes? You're not fourteen, you're an adult. Don't weigh yourself too much and don't wear tiny clothes, and that's half the battle won.

Other advice? Get help quickly. Be honest with yourself—you know if you have a problem; don't wait until you've lost nearly half your body weight like I did. Like drug addiction, like any bad habit, anorexia becomes ingrained; the longer you're underweight the harder it is to recover.

And when you're trying to gain weight, eat whatever you can. In an ideal world everyone's diet would be the perfect balance of carbohydrates, proteins, and fats, but don't worry about it. I have a fat phobia but I crave healthy stuff—I'd never be able to eat fried food but I can cope with carbs. If you like chocolate, eat it; if you love baked beans from the can, or toast and jam, that's fine too. If you're better with those high-calorie drinks or milkshakes, fill your boots. Don't worry about balance at the moment, just get the calories in. In terms of nutrition, a few months of Jell-O and ice cream will not do any long-term damage.

Be kind to yourself. A cliché, yes, but important. Drink wine if you like it, have hot bubble baths, go to the cinema, find activities that absorb you. For me it's writing; for you it could be singing or learning a new language. The more interests you have that are unrelated to food or exercise, the more of your identity you preserve from anorexia. For years I devoted my life to self-punishment: sub-zero runs at dawn, starvation, isolation, hurting myself with men who didn't love me, abandoning men who did. Stop the internal warfare; it doesn't get you anywhere.

As well as eating *whatever* you can, eat *however* you can. Don't worry if your methods are abnormal. If you need people around to distract you, eat with others. If you prefer to eat alone, that's OK too. A few years ago I found eating in public so difficult I'd eat on a bench in Regent's Park, even in winter. I simply couldn't cope with lunch at the office.

Delete the word "greed" from your vocabulary. Don't allow eating to become an emotional battleground of want and worth; stop feeling guilty about it. Remember, your brain and internal organs need food to function properly. Try to be strict with yourself and just fuel your body the way you put gas in the car. Anorexics have phenomenal willpower; now you need to turn that willpower to your advantage. You've proved you can starve yourself, now it's time to make up some new rules.

As well as good nutrition and professional help, you need emotional support. Keep reaching out and asking for help (I'm bad at this). Don't isolate yourself, don't hide away. Join things, visit places, maintain physical contact with the world, go for a massage or give yourself one. At my sickest I avoided human touch (it made me want to cry), but trust me, you need lots of hugs. And by the way, when the ability to cry returns, it feels amazing.

Don't get too deeply involved in online forums. The more time you spend discussing the illness on message boards, the less time you're out in the real world, meeting real people, getting on with life, and the more the anorexia will come to define you. Similarly, I avoid group therapy, although individual therapy has been invaluable. For me, online anorexia groups and websites quickly become a world in themselves—they can encourage comparison with other, sicker sufferers and can even trigger worse habits—but this is just my personal opinion; you may find them helpful.

Invent your reason to get better. Dream up a goal or reward: a country you want to visit, a baby you want to have, anything that galvanizes you. You need something greater than the illness to beat it.

Finally (and this is slightly paradoxical) remember that nothing is irrevocable. Treat your recovery like an experiment. Just try gaining weight for once, see what a difference it makes to your mental and physical well-being. Every pound you are able to put on will help the healing process. If you really hate it, you can lose all the weight again, but for now just try eating, try being well.

* * *

Not exactly rocket science, but after everything I've tried in the ongoing fight against anorexia, this is the essence of what helped me.

When it comes to professional treatment, I can't pretend that anything "worked" for me. As I've said, I believe the most important step in recovery is actually wanting to get out into the world again, really longing to be well—not just saying it to your doctors and parents but meaning it, in your heart. Anorexia may have the highest mortality rate of any mental illness, but this isn't cancer or AIDS we're talking about here: in the vast majority of cases, if you decide it and fight for it and start to eat and keep at it, you can recover. The personal decision is half the battle. Having said that, I wouldn't disregard professional intervention. I've had my fair share of it.

At Oxford, where the weight loss kicked off, I had what was called "counseling." These were weekly sessions with a kindly college nurse who weighed me each week and looked worried when the scale dipped below 84 pounds and kept falling. I remember the excruciation of sitting in the waiting room with the other girls from college; they were waiting for the morning-after pill or a flu shot, and they all knew why I was there. Nurse Brenda, a pudgy lady in her sixties, would ask, "How's your appetite this week, duck?" and I just sat there and felt numb. I'm not sure she had any experience with eating disorders.

Three years later, back in London, I had six months of psychoanalysis at the Tavistock Clinic. This was probably the most traumatic experience of my life, psychologically speaking. I'd been referred to the Tavistock a few weeks after Greg's suicide (because my GP was concerned about my sudden bereavement and concurrent weight loss). The evil psychoanalyst, a cold bitch from some kind of Jungian nightmare, dressed in brown silk with frightening black kohl eyeliner, sat in the corner and stared at me for what felt like hours on end. For the first three weeks— each session lasting ninety minutes—she said nothing, not a single word. It's surprising how this gets to you. Finally, halfway through week three, I began to cry (from the strain of it all, I suppose) and she continued to stare at me silently. It was as if she had to break me down before she would start to do her job, whatever that was. The interaction (I won't call it a conversation) began once I was "broken," but we never approached anything like a trusting or helpful relationship. The woman questioned and then overturned everything I believed in: my happy childhood, my grief at Greg's death, my desire to recover from anorexia. I have never felt so wretched or alone as I did on that couch at the Tavistock. I find I haven't been able to think about it directly for years, but I've remained somewhat distrustful of the manipulative, bullying nature of traditional psychoanalysis. Of course I was in a bad way—vulnerable and bereaved—but surely therapy should not destroy you without rebuilding you? I'm still not sure what she hoped to achieve.

Next was Pramjit, the lovely eating disorders specialist I saw for many years. Our sessions took the form of cognitive behavioral therapy (CBT), in which both faulty thinking (cognitions) and unhelpful behaviors (food dodging) are addressed. It's a proactive approach, based on challenging one's own negative assumptions, breaking out of repetitive, damaging cycles and establishing new behavior patterns. With CBT, I found myself starting to be honest about what I was thinking. Why not be honest? It wasn't anything Pramjit hadn't heard before, and what was the point of pretending I wasn't struggling? I had to admit to all the missed meals, I had to explain why I hadn't eaten that week, what the actual barriers were day-to-day; I had to try to discuss how I might incorporate food into daily life. We would set tangible goals: I would attend the office party and "enjoy" the Christmas dinner, I would try to eat a slice of cake on my birthday. I usually failed but sometimes succeeded.

Treatment with Pramjit was "holistic," encompassing many aspects of recovery. As well as our weekly CBT sessions, family therapy was suggested (my parents were not keen). Sometimes I had a homeopathic massage with a chatty Irishwoman called Jeannie. Often I had "menu planning" sessions with Marianne the dietitian. (Those food diaries always went in the trash.)

Pramjit was kind and sympathetic, and we grew quite close, but it didn't get me eating again. I watched as she got engaged, then married, and finally left to have her first baby—all while I was stuck in my anorexic cage—and wondered if I'd ever get free.

Without doubt the most effective treatment was my former psychiatrist Dr. Robinson. He retired last year, but for eight years I visited his offices once a fortnight.

* * *

Dr. Paul Robinson was my consultant at the Royal Free Hospital in North London. Every other Tuesday I would start work at 7 AM so that I could leave a few hours early. I'd kept it vague with colleagues: only my assistant and the department secretary were aware that I had a regular commitment out of the office on these days. I'd had to explain to my boss, of course, but I didn't go into detail about what kind of doctor's appointment it was, just that I was requesting flexitime once a fortnight. Whatever they may say to the contrary, big corporations get very nervous about employees with mental health issues.

It's weird being a "functioning anorexic." Quite often, in the midst of a hectic Tuesday, I'd wonder why I was going to see Dr. Robinson at all. I didn't feel particularly anorexic rushing around the office—or rather I did, but that was normal to me, not something that needed addressing at that particular point in a busy working day. When I was up against a printer's deadline, checking last-minute proofs or trying to finish off the financial papers for the acquisitions committee, going to see my shrink seemed kind of irrelevant. No matter that it was a medical appointment, no matter that I'd started work hours early, every Tuesday afternoon that I slunk out of the office I felt guilty. Now I know how working mothers feel when they leave to collect their children: there's just something about walking past everyone else at their desks that makes you feel like a slacker, without fail. Anyway, I'd get on my bike and cycle from Euston Road to Highgate trying to get out of work mode and into treatment mode in my head. The Royal Free Hospital is perched at the top of Haverstock Hill. For each appointment I cycled up that hill, one of the steepest in London, to a place where I was being told to eat more and exercise less. Even burly men get off and push their bikes up that hill, but of course I wouldn't, even in a force-ten gale, because anorexia means never admitting defeat.

Arriving at the Royal Free Hospital, it felt odd locking up my bike and climbing the stairs (anorexics always take the stairs) to the Adult Psychiatry Unit on the third floor. Wearing pinstriped trousers, a crisp shirt in pale pink or blue, and high-heeled black boots, I looked totally out of place. Many of the girls were inpatients, so they shuffled down the corridors in slippers and PJs; who was I to breeze in here, quite a few pounds heavier than they were, all business suit and fresh air and ruddy cheeks from my bike ride? One afternoon, standing in the corridor taking a work call on my cell, a young man crept past me and I noticed his arms were covered in livid, fresh razor cuts.

God, I felt so "well"—and I mean that in the sense of fat (as in when someone tells you you're looking *well*, and they mean *ample, bouncing, plump*). I was convinced they could all see what a fake I was, how fraudulent my so-called anorexia was. If I was really sick then why had I scarfed that entire banana at lunchtime? I've always felt deeply uneasy around fellow anorexics, and for me the Eating Disorders Unit waiting room of the Adult Psychiatry Department was torture. I know that many sufferers feel the same way—it's almost as if we can read each other's shameful secrets. Just once in all the years I was there did I see a terribly obese woman—Eating Disorder Units treat those with obesity as well as anorexia—and her discomfort was truly awful. She stared at the floor, ashamed to meet anyone's eyes, clearly going through far worse horrors than I was in that waiting room . . . All in all, it was a relief to be called in to see Dr. Robinson.

It's perhaps an indicator of our good relationship that I was able, many times, to walk into his office and say, "I feel a complete fraud next to all your skinny girls." No matter that Dr. Robinson is a rather formal, old-school psychiatrist, no matter that he shuffled those case files around so that I never knew whether he quite remembered who the hell I was—despite that, he was frank with me and I was with him.

I remember our very first appointment, when he kept me waiting for an hour and a half. By the time he called me in I was quite seriously pissed off. I soon got used to it—he gave each patient far longer than the inadequate ten-minute slots allocated by the health care system so his appointments were always running ludicrously late. (I used to wonder whether he was still there at 9 PM, catching up with his afternoon appointments.) I soon learned to take a good book and to turn up an hour after the scheduled time.

This prolonged delay also enabled patients to consume the requisite three or four bottles of water. Water-loading is one of the techniques we used—as well as coins and keys in pockets, wearing thick socks and heavy belts—to artificially boost our weight before climbing onto the scale. It was tricky, waiting hours with a bursting bladder, but a couple of liters of Evian can add precious pounds to your weight chart.

Despite being hopeless at timekeeping, Paul Robinson was also one of the leading specialists in the field of eating disorders. After my experience at the Tavistock Clinic I was wary of all mental health professionals—whether psychologist, psychiatrist, or psychoanalyst—but I was very lucky to have been referred to him. There is good and bad news with this illness, and Dr. Robinson was honest with me from the start. Unlike other eating disorders counselors I'd seen over the years—with their kind words and gentle encouragement—he didn't offer me cups of tea or boxes of Kleenex, and he didn't allow me to feel powerless about anorexia. Indeed, I often felt I was wasting his time. I suppose I was wasting his time, and my time too, sitting in his office, talking about gaining weight and continuing to starve myself. But he never saw me as a hopeless case: he knew and I knew that I could beat anorexia. I think it was his no-nonsense, scientific approach that helped more than anything. I'm someone who prefers to know the facts, however scary they might be—hoping, I suppose, to scare myself into action. Dr. Robinson always told me the truth.

I had not menstruated for years, which meant that I was probably not ovulating, which explains why I am currently infertile. But the good news was that this was mostly reversible. Almost all women with anorexia regain their fertility when they return to a normal weight. When I first started seeing Dr. Robinson, the fertility thing was never my main concern. As I sit here, aged thirty-three, I realize that in my twenties it didn't bother me at all. Sure, the absence of periods was an indication that all was not well, but who really minds not having periods? It only began to bother me when I turned thirty. The weird thing is I never seriously imagined not having children. Was that colossal self-deceit, my mind shutting itself off to the facts? I always assumed it would work itself out in the end.

Dr. Robinson was a good doctor in another way too, in that he referred me for regular tests. One of the most important was the DEXA (dual-emission X-ray absorptiometry), a scan that measures bone mineral density. It's well known that being underweight and without periods is a major risk factor for osteoporosis, but I only recently found out that up to 90 percent of anorexics will show some degree of bone loss. And so it was with me: the DEXAs revealed I had osteopenia (the precursor to full-blown osteoporosis) in my left hip and spine, and my T-scores were deteriorating over the years. How foolish: to be confronted with the truth, the proof of what I was doing to myself, that I could see the frightening results of those bone scans, and still not give up anorexia. While Dr. Robinson's tests didn't cure me, they sure as hell reminded me of the invisible damage anorexia was doing—and more importantly he reminded me that I could do something about it. For women, the twenties are a crucial life stage for building bone mass—perhaps I couldn't reverse the damage completely but I could have helped myself a little more. Except, of course, I couldn't. As always, anorexia was stronger.

Along with the gone-to-sleep ovaries and crumbling-spine charts, Dr. Robinson and I would have discussions about the nature of selfhood and denial, control and sexuality, femininity and family. I would sometimes talk about wanting children and he'd say, "But do you really want to be a mother, Emma?" He would call me on lazy assumptions I was making, he would catch me up when I wasn't being honest with myself. It's easy to *say* you want children—that's what most girls are brought up to say—but it's a lot harder to think about why, and how it might not be easy, or to admit that you have doubts. Even now, writing about my desire to get pregnant in a national newspaper, I still have real fears about how life will change with a baby and the freedom I'll have to give up.

For a bearded, middle-class, gray-suited man in his late fifties, Dr. Robinson seemed to have an instinctive understanding of women: of eating and anxiety and bodies and babies. I talked to him as easily as I might to talk to my mother—more honestly perhaps. Whether I was gaining or losing weight (and mostly I was losing), I just found our sessions intensely interesting.

One Tuesday afternoon in early November, he casually observed that in the Middle Ages I might have been a nun, an ascetic devoted to denying the demands of the flesh. I knew instantly what he meant (I have always identified with Dorothea Brooke in *Middlemarch*). We talked about this many times—the pain and reward of self-denial, and why it appealed to me.

It was raining heavily as I left the hospital, but I cycled home in a trance. All the way, I thought of the medieval literature I'd studied at Oxford; I conjured up vivid images of Julian of Norwich, Margery Kempe, those nuns and mystics mortifying the flesh, starving and praying in their lonely cells. Dr. Robinson had identified something about me I'd never realized: that the anorexia (even more than thinness) satisfies a yearning for something clean and empty. A part of me fears being womanly, fleshy, excessive: I like to be lithe and compact, I like my tone and muscle. I like to run for miles and feel that I am contained in a neat, athlete's body. Being a woman is messy: being a woman involves blood and fat. Anorexia seems very pure and I like that.

I've since found out that my "purity" feeling does make sense. There was a research study in Ghana several years ago that investigated secondary school girls with abnormally low body weight (Bennett et al., *The British Journal of Psychiatry*, 2004). None of these underweight girls displayed a desire to be thin or a morbid fear of fatness—and, even weirder, none reported amenorrhoea. The study reports that they viewed their food restriction positively and in religious terms; they believed in self-control and denial of hunger, but without the typical anorexic concerns over weight and shape. In other words the Ghanaian girls didn't have any problem with body image; they just wanted to be more religious and holy.

Although Dr. Robinson didn't ultimately cure me, I enjoyed exploring these cultural and social ideas with him, ideas beyond the usual bland eating disorders narratives. It's important to have some insight into what is, after all, a serious mental illness. I have lived with this for a third of my life. For me it's normal, but it makes normal life impossible. Succumbing to hunger is weak: that is the basic rule by which I live. After thirty years in the field, Dr. Robinson understands this. It's a relief to be able to talk about it, when so much of this illness is secrecy and deception.

There would come a point, for all our talk, when I would have to shut up and be weighed. The fear of not gaining weight and the much greater fear of gaining would crystallize into those few moments where he would close my file and say, "Right, let's weigh you." I would slip off my shoes or unzip my boots and step onto the digital scale in the corner of his office.

The scales in Eating Disorder Units are terrifyingly precise. They are checked and recalibrated once a week—I imagine only the grand pianos in the Royal Opera House have as much fine-tuning. I was aware of them throughout every appointment, those terrible scales, crouched in the corner, waiting to judge me. *I step onto the scale and everything goes silent, I close my eyes and open them slowly, and watch the green digits flicker up and down, 101, 104, 105, 103 . . . before they settle and flash twice and hold, pronouncing on my fate, whether I am a failure, whether I am a winner. For however much I tell myself that it's not about the numbers, it's not about my physical weight, at some level it is.* So he would weigh me and note down the numbers in my notes, and compare it to the previous fortnight's tally, and we'd discuss why I wasn't making progress. Again he would explain what I had to do, and again I would promise to do it.

The longer I failed to make progress, the more embarrassing it became. I remember one appointment very clearly: it was my twenty-ninth birthday. I'd somehow dropped a few extra pounds that week—as a birthday present to myself, or perhaps it was linked to me giving up smoking. Apparently cigarettes speed up your metabolism; apparently giving them up makes you feel hungrier and eat lots and pile on the pounds. Yet, petrified of gaining weight post-cigarettes, convinced that my nicotine-deprived metabolism would grind to a halt, I had been compensating by eating even less than usual. I was half-crazed with Marlboro Light withdrawal, edgy as a junkie, and a few pounds lighter, drifting down under 100 pounds again. At the end of the session as I stood up to leave, Dr. Robinson looked me straight in the eye and said, "It's time to give up the anorexia, Emma. It's time to grow up." I felt so ashamed.

* * *

Although anorexia is a solitary illness, it's also competitive. No-where was that more apparent to me than in the Eating Disorders Unit. Despite being an overwhelmingly female condition, it's not a cozy sisterhood, not like those friendly Weight Watchers groups where women trade dieting tips and fat-free chocolate cake reci-pes. Of course weight-loss groups may be competitive too, but they seem to foster a sense of camaraderie that has no parallel in the world of anorexia. You gather a bunch of anorexic women together in the depressing lounge of the therapy suite, all purple sofas and "balanced meal" charts on the wall, and they glance at each other—and that's when you feel fatter or thinner, that's when the guilt and the comparisons begin. When I wrote a column one week, warning other sufferers against getting involved in group therapy, I received some fairly vitriolic responses from practicing therapists. I understand—they believe that group settings can be beneficial—but I disagree.

For me, group therapy simply made matters worse. Whenever I tried it, the inpatients would scrutinize me, comparing my level of thinness to their own. I have felt it so many times, that anorexic flick up and down the body, assessing you in one quick glance. To be taken seriously, your thighs must be like twigs, your arms like matchsticks. Any hint of flesh or softness and you are automatically dismissed. I don't remember anyone ever chatting in the waiting room before or after group sessions. I don't remember meeting anyone's eyes.

Although I may have felt uncomfortable as an outpatient, a fat fraud, I never wanted to be a part of the inpatient world. Those hollow girls were the hard core. Ranging in age from early teens to late forties, they spent every day in the unit. Each meal was measured and monitored, the patients ever vigilant to see who was eating and exactly how much. Every hour of the day was filled with therapeutic activities or group sessions, until your illness became your identity. In my opinion, this is the risk of becoming an inpatient: that soon you have nothing left but anorexia.

Maybe that's why, even when my weight had dropped below 80 pounds, I fought against hospitalization like a drowning cat tied in a sack. I was focusing on my finals at Oxford, then my career: was I expected to leave my job, go into the hospital, and be force-fed? I always felt that becoming an inpatient would be the beginning of the end. Maybe I was wrong—maybe if I'd surrendered to radical intervention at an earlier stage I would be free of anorexia today. But as long as I live, I'll never forget the holocaust levels of starvation I've seen in Eating Disorder Units. (It's been estimated that many anorexics survive on less than 800 calories a day—I've done it myself—which is well below the average caloric intake of a Belsen concentration camp inmate.) If only the psychologists, the art and music therapists, and the dietitians could know what it's like from the inside, how it feels to be in these units, the way their patients constantly look and compare. What could be more dangerous for anorexics than to compare their own body and food intake with other anorexics? This is why I believe that these groups can do more harm than good.

Anorexia is at the extreme end of this spectrum, of course, but it's a spectrum most women are familiar with. We may deny it, but women judge other women's bodies far more harshly than men do, both in the media and in our own lives. I'm not the first woman to point out that most of the female angst about female bodies and weight and appearance is caused by our own or other women's expectations—not those of men. As I've said before, we're our own worst enemies. While we're passing judgment on that extra roll of fat or that dimpled hint of cellulite, men are feasting their eyes on a curvy female figure.

Despite my antipathy to group therapy, I do have friends with eating disorders. I "met" some amazing people on the BBC Health message boards (now sadly defunct), most of whom I'm still in contact with. But although I feel I know them—Sunray and Hannah and Kitty and Vics—I've never met them and I don't want to. The Internet can offer a safe, nonjudgmental anonymity. Others have emailed since I started writing the column, and we "chat" quite openly on-screen: Sarah is head of a global division at a major international bank; Rachel is a mother of three and lives in Birmingham; Cara is a primary school teacher—they're all out there, living their lives with anorexia. I could walk past them in the street and not know them, but we have shared our most private struggles. We couldn't have become that close if we knew each other in person. Anorexia just doesn't work like that. With anorexia, you triumph when others gain weight and you don't. The infamous Gore Vidal quote captures it perfectly: "It is not enough to succeed. Others must fail." The schadenfreude in anorexia is like nothing else . . .

* * *

As I mentioned before, out of everything I tried, it was therapy with Dr. Robinson that helped the most. Quite simply, it helped me understand, and start to challenge, the anorexic trap in which I was caught. Our sessions taught me that, beyond the simple facts of food and weight, anorexia was serving some kind of purpose for me. Yes, there were benefits, otherwise why would I carry on? I found this troubling to come to terms with at first, that such an idiotic mental illness could possibly confer any benefits . . . but it's true. Even though I claim to hate my anorexia, there must be a good reason why I have not been able to let it go.

At the heart of this struggle is, of course, control. For some reason I don't trust myself or my appetite; I fear that if I "let go" and eat, I'll go wildly out of control. I don't know where this comes from. Anorexia is an excellent way to avoid getting fully involved in life, and a way of being unkind to myself.

This is something Dr. Robinson pointed out to me quite soon after I started attending his clinic. It was a wet and gusty day and I'd arrived by bike, as usual. He asked, casually, whether I ever considered taking the tube or the bus, "Most cyclists give up the bike in the harshest winter months—why not give yourself a break, just when it's freezing cold or raining or snowing out? You could stay warm, use public transport instead." I looked at him, confused. The thought hadn't occurred to me. And so we began to explore the idea of punishment.

On a bitter winter's morning in London, I would make myself stand under an ice-cold shower. I was still doing that in October, November, right up until I began to turn things around at the end of last year. Why would I do that? Simple: it hurts. It isn't a punishment exactly, but more what the opposite implies: a warm bath or hot shower implies comfort and ease and, yes, neediness. I don't do it so much anymore—part of this challenge has been about learning to be kinder to myself, and I'm getting better at that—but once in a while, when I'm getting lazy or complacent, I'll remind myself that I'm still sharp with a painfully cold shower, or a day without food. The human need for comfort seems like weakness to me. I am wary of those needs—warmth and food and love—because once you start where does it end? You start to *rely on* softness and company and other people's love. I'm not needy or greedy, I'm fine and I can manage alone. When Laurie left me, I didn't go running to him, begging him to take me back—I just dealt with it. When Greg killed himself—I just dealt with it. No one is ever going to accuse me of *needing* things; I'm OK on my own. People leave you, people die: what can you rely on, really?

Far better to stay on your guard, far better to know that you can cope when things go wrong.

* * *

Turns out there are many ways to punish yourself. For me, running came late on, but once discovered I threw myself into it completely. Dr. Robinson looked concerned when I took up running. My parents didn't like it when I took up running. My big sister looked wary when I took up running. Running was central to my self-punishment regime—and this is why I miss it so much. I remember my last long Sunday morning run, seven months ago now. I was halfway through a fast 10K and overtook some women on the canal towpath running (or rather "jogging") together. I wondered, *Why would you run with someone else?* Why would you choose to share this intense, solitary activity, mile after mile, in sunshine and rain, alone with your thoughts, every step making you leaner, firmer, every mile taking you farther from the lazy, lethargic world? Like writing and eating, I couldn't stand to share my running. It was such a personal thing: a therapeutic punishment, a way to push, push, push myself.

I had stopped smoking one day and started running the next, telling myself it would help me recover, that this new "healthy" regime was a fresh start. I had read magazine articles where former anorexics talked about how regular exercise helped them overcome the illness. But for me, running was absolutely feeding the eating disorder. When I vowed to start eating more then I would run more, five or ten miles in a day, on top of the long bike ride to and from work. Sometimes I would get up at 5 AM and run through the city, along the Thames, criss-crossing Tower Bridge, London Bridge, Southwark Bridge, Waterloo Bridge.

When Dr. Robinson first told me about "jogger's infertility" I hadn't actually heard the term before but my body immediately got it. Research has shown that the beta-endorphins induced by intense exercise—the endorphins that produce the post-run euphoria— also act to suppress the ovaries. Runners are literally pounding their ovaries into submission. Just what I needed, another way to attack my nonfunctioning reproductive system. He told me about the "athletic triad": amenorrhoea, osteoporosis, anorexia. Maybe those risks are worth it for an athlete, ballerina, or marathon runner earning her living through this damaging lifestyle, but I'm not.

I don't know why I loved running so much, and I don't know why I took to hunger so proficiently. I have been trying to focus on this and nothing else, to understand why I'd want to hurt myself, what I'm unhappy about, what punishment gives me.

Something about self-denial sharpens my sense of self. And after so long, it has come to define me; this is what I am, this is what I do. Of course there's everything else—my writing, my family, my relationship with Tom, my flat—but the eating disorder is part of my identity. I fear that when the anorexia is gone, something huge will be missing. The logical solution, which I'm trying to talk myself into, is to find something else. If I need to fill the missing gap, fill it with something constructive, something less self-destructive. In the same way that running replaced smoking, could being a mother replace being an anorexic?

* * *

Despite my skepticism, it turns out that psychological treatment can provide important insights and a level of self-understanding. Now, more than a year since our final session, Dr. Robinson and I are in contact again. After the first column in *The Times*, he emailed out of the blue. When it landed in my in-box, it was like receiving a message from the Queen.

Dear Emma,

Wow. I was so impressed to read your article, but quite stunned to read that you are going to do it! I can imagine you must feel apprehensive, but it could well work, after so long trying. I wish you all the best in the world—I've even taken out a subscription to TimesOnline *to follow your progress.*

It still sounds hard for you and I was wondering what doing this in the public gaze does? What it says to me is that the part of you that wants to beat the anorexia is saying, "Get out there and show them!" while the side that still holds onto thinness must be really terrified of that publicity, all that exposure. Demons that visit us in the night melt away with the morning light. Perhaps you are hoping (perhaps with reason) that the anorexia demon will be weakened by being exposed.

I've got to know so many patients with anorexia (to encourage you, one just sent me a photo of her new baby) and of those who recovered (sadly not all did as you know from your clinic visits), the ways they recovered were really diverse. One set her sights on a job and knew that the anorexia was standing in her way. Another wanted to be a mother and managed to overcome some awful experiences from adolescence and move on. The most remarkable was a woman in her forties who had anorexia since nineteen and had nearly died from starvation. She started putting on weight and completely recovered over about a year. I asked her what had made the difference. She said, "Do you remember me asking you, 'How can I escape from this awful thing?' and you said, 'Why don't you try eating a little more?'" I don't know what to make of that, but maybe she needed permission to feel less guilty about satisfying her hunger.

After having heard all these thousands of stories I (shamefully) still can't answer the question about what works. Sometimes I think that anorexia is a circuitous route through a minefield. The mines differ for each person. In some they are memories of abuse, in others, diverse traumas. Sometimes you get free of the minefield and can walk straighter; some, sadly, don't. I'm sure in many cases we don't even know what the mines are, and maybe they are, or become, imaginary. I would suggest that that might be the case with you, Emma. If the anorexia is a cupboard you are sitting in to avoid the dangers outside, perhaps the only way to find out if they are real or not is to come out of the cupboard and see. You may well find that your imagined demons dissolve when you work up the courage to face them.

In any case, congratulations for your excellent and courageous project. I'm sure there are many people (including me) rooting for you to succeed.

Dr. Robinson

I had been nervous, writing about my psychiatrist. Admitting that he hadn't cured me seemed ungracious in the extreme, like impugning his professional skills. So it was a great relief to hear that Dr. Robinson was behind me in this project. Since then we've corresponded regularly by email—I actually feel more comfortable with him now than I did in eight years of face-to-face consultations—and he's happy to answer my endless questions about anorexia, recovery, and conception.

A few months ago I was seriously considering fertility treatment. There are many slim women out there who manage to have babies despite their low body weight, and I've been getting so frustrated that I can't do the same. Thirty-three isn't old, but it isn't young either, on the fertility timeline. I long to get things moving. I did a lot of research on the Internet, and also talked to two older female friends about it, both of whom took Clomiphene decades ago, and both of whom have had breast cancer since. I spoke to Tom about it, who was excited and supportive at first, and then unsure when we looked at the risk factors. I spoke to my mum, who was absolutely against it, because of the possible cancer link. Eventually I emailed Dr. Robinson for a considered medical opinion:

It's much better, and healthier, to start your cycle naturally rather than use hormones. It's possible that if you're still doing a lot of exercise, you may have increased your muscle-to-fat ratio, and that can prolong the time, and increase the weight you need, before you get periods. Remember, the body's thinking behind the decision to switch on the ovaries is:

- *Is there enough energy stored (i.e., fat) to feed a baby through the nine months of pregnancy? and*
- *Is there enough fat stored to allow the mother to produce milk after the birth? This rationale is not interested in muscle. Muscle is for running after mammoths. (That may seem very non-PC but I don't think Bernard Biology has feminism as a priority philosophy: babies, yes; women in the front line of battle, not really.)*

Best wishes,
Dr. Robinson

In other words, in a biological sense, women need fat. Mother Nature does not care about muscle tone or skinny jeans or size zeros, not when it comes to making a baby. No amount of fruit or bread or cereal can substitute for solid reproductive building blocks. Fat triggers the hormones that trigger ovulation and conception and breast-feeding and cuddling. Fat prepares the uterus as a cozy nest for the embryo.

And fat is the thing I fear above all else.

Chapter 9
On the Road

"You could be closer than you think."

A ll it takes is a single egg, one healthy egg to be released (plus the miracle of conception) and we could have the makings of a baby. I've had all the tests, my blood results are healthy, my FSH (follicle stimulating hormone) isn't elevated, my ovarian reserve is good, and all other hormonal levels are normal. Next step is an ultrasound scan of my ovaries.

It's the start of May and I'm at home, packing for a trip to the States, when the letter from my doctor drops through the door.

Dear Miss Woolf,

Following your recent blood tests, I can confirm that nothing abnormal has been detected. This is an encouraging set of results. I have now made a referral to the Royal Free Hospital for your ovarian scan, as requested. It is good news that you have managed to increase your weight; the results suggest to me that you may be close to ovulating. The process is impossible to predict with accuracy—as you know, the body is not a computer—but you could be closer than you think.

I'm over the moon as I dial Tom's cell number. Everything's healthy, and I could be close to ovulating. We could be close to the possibility of conceiving. Surely this is enough to make me eat?

* * *

The next day we're on the road, driving from Denver to San Francisco. Fifteen days, thirteen cities, ten hotels, 2,000 miles; even for travel junkies like me and Tom this is quite some trip. And, as everyone keeps telling me, America is the ideal place to "super-size" myself (a comment that causes me serious alarm).

We fly into Denver, the Mile High City, in the early hours of a Wednesday in the midst of a snowstorm. With a four-hour layover in Washington, D.C., we've been traveling for nearly twenty-four hours and we're aching all over: knees, back, and shoulders. "I swear the blood is pooling in my legs, my feet are like lead," Tom murmurs as we stand at the baggage carousel. "Me too," I say. "My head feels like a cannonball, too heavy for my neck."

It's a long journey but we hold it together relatively well. There's a minor meltdown situation near the very end, in the car rental offices, but that's understandable. It's nearly 2 AM local time when we clear customs and collect our luggage, so the National Car Rental offices are closed, with only a sign directing customers to report to Alamo Rental Services. This appears to be in another terminal entirely, and we find ourselves dragging heavy suitcases up and down the interminable airport concourses. When we find Alamo, by this point shivering in our thin sweaters, we wait twenty-five minutes in the snow for anyone to appear from inside the locked building.

At long last, after paperwork and insurance and driving license and credit card checks (both of us close to collapse behind the counter), we are sent out into the deserted parking lot, with the instructions that we can choose "any compact or sport vehicle, Mustang through Oldsmobile, excepting hybrid and ultra versions." Planning the road trip back home, we'd had excited discussions about the ideal car for these thousands of miles, but in my exhaustion, frankly, I couldn't care less. It is pitch black and at least ten degrees below, making it difficult to distinguish one model from another. We stagger around, our suitcase wheels hopeless in the snow drifts, wiping the ice from the back of cars with frozen fingers, working out which is which. By this point it is nearing 10 AM U.K. time and we are cold, tired, and very hungry. Predictably I hadn't eaten much on the journey—I find airline food impossible—although I smuggled my usual apple on board and Tom brought a bunch of bananas. The car selection process is hard to care about when you're as ravenous as I am. I lean against a boxy little 4 x 4, muttering, "How about this one?" while Tom locates something more suitable for our epic journey . . . a convertible Mustang.

It gets us to our hotel that night, where we rouse the night porter with a doorbell, and are given the keys to a bedroom on the eighteenth floor. Floor-to-ceiling windows promise stunning views, but we are too tired to gaze out at downtown Denver glittering in the night below us; we stumble into the bedroom and look at each other, dazed with relief. It is warm, it is cozy, and, finally, we can drop our suitcases and kick off our shoes . . . The carpet is soft and thick beneath our feet, there are two huge double beds, the bathroom is tiny but spotlessly clean. There is also an orange goldfish flitting around in a large glass bowl, which for some reason spooks us, so we put it outside on a table in the hallway.

We pull back the fresh white sheets on one of the beds and Tom runs me a bath. Dropping my clothes on the floor, I submerge myself in the hot water, while Tom collapses onto the bed . . .

Within ten minutes I am curled in his arms in a damp towel I am too tired to unwind, and then we are both asleep.

And in the morning we discover our convertible Mustang is a fabulous fire-engine red.

Tom is writing a travel feature to coincide with the movie of Jack Kerouac's *On The Road*; I'm writing and doing research, so we're glued to our notebooks wherever we go, diving into museums and local heritage centers, always hunting for that extra detail, the story that might bring a town to life.

Between us, Tom and I keep the Moleskine company afloat: my notebooks are various rainbow colors (this one is turquoise) and Tom's are always black. His reporter's notebooks go back twenty years, since he started in journalism, and he's like a cold-turkey drug addict without them. Once every few days he has a "lost notebook" crisis; then we have to turn the hotel room upside down, gut the car, empty the suitcases, retrace our steps to the previous gas station—and then we find it tucked neatly in the side of his camera case or jacket pocket.

* * *

I've never been this far west. I've lived in New York, and I've traveled on Greyhound buses all over the Deep South, but never across to the West Coast. I can't wait to explore Saratoga, Sausalito, Sacramento, San Francisco. I love the names.

After two days in Denver, we head into the heart of Colorado's Rocky Mountains. In Central City we stay in the only hotel in town: Century City Casino, a faded warehouse of a building with all the glitz flaking off. It's sadder than you can imagine, this broken-down assortment of loners and losers, alcoholics and old folk, gambling their pensions, cashing in their social security checks, pouring their savings and homes and marriages into the greedy slot machines. There's no skill or glamour to this kind of gambling: it's nickels and quarters rattling down the slots, plastic money bags; it's sick people shuffling around in slippers, an old woman with a dialysis machine attached to her wheelchair, an old man pulling his IV drip and catheter bag on a frame as he drags on a cigarette and feeds in the pennies.

Around 7 AM we go downstairs for breakfast—have you ever eaten in the restaurant of a casino? It's a canteen, reeking of fried food; the plates and even the cutlery are plastic. Every booth shows another hopeless human story: the middle-aged cowboy couple, anxiously counting their loose change; the young mother and father smoking, arguing, with three little children; the obese man ploughing his way through platefuls of egg and sausage and fried bread.

I take one look at the "menu"—option 1 is fried breakfast; option 2 is short-stack pancakes and maple syrup; option 3 is waffles and jelly—and nip back upstairs to collect a banana and a yogurt. Tom orders scrambled eggs "over easy," bacon and fried tomatoes. We sit there, smiling at each other, dazed by our jet lag and the unreal scenes around us. I've never been to a casino before, so after breakfast Tom insists we have a flutter. The blackjack tables are closed, so we change up ten dollars and head for the slot machines; even at 8 AM the casino is full. After losing $9 straight, we win $60 on our final $1 bet . . . jackpot! Of course we're hooked—and it's tempting to continue—but I drag Tom away from the slots and out of the casino. Even this kind of minor win is heady, but I don't need a gambling addiction as well as an eating disorder. And anyway, we have 290 miles to cover today.

We stay in various casinos on our way through Nevada. If the experience of visiting casinos is eye-opening, it's even weirder staying there. You might expect loud music, drunkenness, and general nocturnal disruption, but they are surprisingly quiet places. The corridors of bedrooms are kept well away from the main gaming rooms, and anyway most of the other guests are occupied at the tables until 4 or 5 AM, if they go to bed at all. Often casinos will give free bedrooms to their best customers, who maybe go for an hour's nap and a shower around dawn, but generally the business of casinos is winning or losing dollars. Why waste time sleeping when your life's savings are waiting to be lost?

As for casino "restaurants"—I don't eat in them, obviously, but even accompanying Tom down to breakfast in the mornings is depressing. Not just the 7 AM gamblers, sad families with children, and desperately ill folk, but the general air of hopelessness. There is no air in a casino: no windows or clocks, so you can't keep track of time, no natural daylight or oxygen. There's little eye contact and people don't talk much.

For me, the breakfast choices at casinos are stomach turning: how can people exist without fresh food in the morning? At the risk of sounding like a middle-class, organic, raw-food hippy, I'll say it anyway—no fruit, no yogurt, no muesli, nothing but options 1, 2, and 3—fried platter, pancakes, eggs and biscuits (I think option 3 is supposed to be the healthy option!). Fortunately the coffee-refilling waitresses don't bat an eyelid at me bringing my own breakfast into the booth—they seem too jaded and world-weary to care. "Y'all come back, ya hear" they always murmur as we leave, but their hearts aren't really in it . . .

If casino catering falls somewhat short of my orthorexic obses-sion with pure and unadulterated food, American supermarkets more than make up for it. We stop regularly along the highways at Walmart, Target, and my personal favorite, Whole Foods. We restock the cooler in the trunk with huge baskets of strawberries and raspberries, luscious, sun-drenched oranges, enormous red apples. It's bewildering, the sheer range of products on offer—not five choices of bread, but ten or twenty (rye, wheat, whole-grain, spelt, sourdough); vast coolers of yogurt; endless aisles of soft drinks, sodas, water, energy water; a million varieties of cereal. Tom keeps himself road-worthy with foot-long subs, some of which contain up to four different kinds of meat: turkey, ham, salami, and chicken. Everything in abundance and—looking at the obese shoppers, their carts piled high with sugar-free, fat-free food, the so-called "lighter options"—you realize that everything is excessive.

"One of these days, Em, you'll have a breakthrough." We're at a gas station two hours outside Boulder, somewhere in the Rockies. "I'll be filling up the car and you'll go inside for sodas, and you'll come back to the car with some Krispy Kreme doughnuts and you'll just eat one." Tom reaches out and puts his arms around me. We stand on the courtyard in the crisp, bright sunshine, delaying the moment when we have to get back in the car. "You'll just eat a lovely doughnut and enjoy it—that's the breakthrough I'm waiting for."

I don't think he knows how far I am from eating a Krispy Kreme doughnut, ever.

* * *

We're driving though Wyoming. My feet are on the dashboard, Tom's at the wheel of our red Mustang. It's been five hours since we left Boulder and we've seen nothing but the highway ahead and the endless, barren prairie. Wyoming is true cowboy country, more than 97,000 square miles and only 500,000 inhabitants. Just to put that in context, the whole of Britain is only 88,000 square miles and has over 62 million inhabitants. We drive and drive and see nothing but the endless road ahead and the big sky and waving prairie grasses. Wyoming feels like 97,000 square miles of emptiness.

Thank God for the radio stations: Bigfoot 99 has kept us going since Colorado, singing along to Emmylou Harris and Woody Guthrie and Dolly Parton, all our latest discoveries. Is this new appreciation of country music a sign of getting old, we discuss at length, as the road unfurls ahead of us. There's "Jolene," "This Land is Your Land," and "Almost Home." There are newer tracks like "Tequila Makes Her Clothes Fall Off," a catchy bluegrass number we know by heart by the time we reach Saratoga.

Saratoga, Wyoming: a one-horse town. Well, there's a small grocery store, a gas station (which looks like it hasn't sold gas since the 1940s), and a trading post selling cowboy boots for cowboys, not tourists. Then, just on the way out of town, tucked into the bend of a river, the Saratoga Hot Springs Resort. We drive in and park outside a small wooden shed with a swinging sign marked RECEPTION. It's nearly 6 PM and we've been driving since morning; flakes of snow swirl around as we wrestle our suitcases out of the trunk.

The motel grounds are floodlit, to illuminate what Saratoga is proudest of: its natural hot springs. It's an extraordinary experience, slipping into the boiling waters from the near-freezing night air. As well as the large rectangular swimming pool, around which the bungalows are arranged, farther off in the darkness is a cluster of tepees atop miniature plunge pools just big enough for one (or two in romantic mood). We float in the sulphurous waters until long after the sun has set, enjoying the therapeutic effects on our car-weary muscles—and soon getting used to the foul sulphurous stench of egg. There is no one else around but we find ourselves talking in whispers. Looking up at the night sky and the millions of tiny stars, it feels like we're the only people on this planet.

Later, over a snack dinner in the homely dining room (fresh granary rolls and a bowl of tomato soup for me, steak and fries and coleslaw for Tom), the owner tells us the waters come from the underground springs in Saratoga . . . "It comes clean outta the ground up to 140 degrees but we make sure to cool it down with the nearby stream." She looks so nicely presented, this lady of a certain age, all neatly permed hair and frosty pink lipstick, even though it's late and out of season and we're her only guests. You want her for your auntie, or an older best girlfriend. She speaks in that correct, slightly formal way Americans have when they're not used to foreigners. "Right now, I'd guess it's about 100 degrees out there . . . maybe somewhat cooler after nightfall." (Later, as we're leaving the dining room, she confides in me, "I sure love your British accent, I could just listen to you folks talk all night.")

* * *

The miles are adding up: five days on the road and we've driven nearly 1,000 miles. At the Colorado–Utah border, we do not see "God in the sky in the form of huge sunbathing clouds above the desert" (as Jack Kerouac did), but we marvel at the steep miles of curving, rolling highway on our descent into Salt Lake City. After the remoteness of Wyoming, SLC is a revelation: stylish and much livelier than we'd expected. Despite its reputation as a "dry" state, we find plenty of bars open. And it must be the cleanest city in the world: walking around town for two days, I didn't see a single piece of trash on the streets, not a wad of chewing gum or even a cigarette butt.

On our first morning we wander a few blocks from our hotel to visit the World Headquarters of the Church of Latter-Day Saints, slap bang in the middle of town. I have to admit, I'm captivated by this whole Mormon thing: elegant temples and glittering gold domes; acres of immaculate grounds, a multi-colored riot of tulips, green lawns, splashing fountains, and gray marble courtyards. There is some secrecy—we're not allowed into the temple buildings—but apart from that we wander freely through the parks. And every Mormon we meet is normal and welcoming: two young women stop and smile, ask if we need directions, offer us a map. They take our photograph by the tulips and recommend a nearby coffee shop with "the best frozen yogurt in Utah." No one talks of God or finding the true path: they are genuinely not trying to indoctrinate us, just saying hello.

And this is a wonderful new experience: frozen yogurt. We find the coffee shop and collapse into a booth at the back. Tom goes up to the counter and comes back with two large tubs: vanilla yogurt topped with blueberries for me, raspberry yogurt topped with strawberries for him. Frozen yogurt is like ice cream (which I haven't eaten since around 1989) and tastes absolutely delicious. It's actually fat-free, but that's not the point: it's a novelty to enjoy eating the same thing as my boyfriend, something fun and unplanned, between meals, just for a treat. I don't do that very often—well, never. We spoon it down greedily as it melts, swapping spoonfuls of raspberry and vanilla. Tom keeps smiling at me.

We roll onwards "balling the jack" like Jack Kerouac, across the blinding Salt Lake flats, where we stop the car and taste lumps of solid rock salt on our tongues. Out of Utah and on across the desert into Nevada, stopping for a night in Elko (a small, dusty casino town) and another night in Reno (a larger, glitzier dusty casino town). Leaving Nevada we stop in Lovelock, another small town, with "one of only two circular courthouses in the U.S." (who knew?), a grocery store, and the town's main attraction: the love-chain. From a stall next to the grocery store we buy a padlock with our names engraved on it: *Tom and Emma, May 2011*. Then we join thousands of previous tourists in locking our cheesy padlock onto the hefty iron chain looped around the courthouse park, thus "locking our love forever."

I don't know about locking our love forever, but the road trip has tested our relationship. There have been tensions and disagreements—inevitable when you're spending eight or nine hours a day driving—but there's also a sense of camaraderie. We're in this together, through so many unfamiliar situations and alien places, and we're looking after each other. It has always felt like this: me and Tom against the world. We argue a lot, but we're also good at recovering: we forgive quickly and put it behind us. My mother used to say, "Never go to bed angry," and I'm starting to learn the truth of this—one of the best ways to resolve a fight is just to take someone's hand in the dark as you drift off to sleep.

* * *

We've been on the road for nine days when we finally reach Lake Tahoe. The trip has been more tiring than we'd expected—nothing but the road ahead and the mountains or valleys, the radio, and oncoming trucks and each other to distract us. We need this break.

Crossing into California the landscape changes: it's instantly lusher and greener. The red rocks of the Nevada Desert are replaced by orange groves, and it's abundant in natural resources, sunshine, and fertile land—you can see why early settlers called it the promised land. Driving into Tahoe we open the car windows to smell the pine trees, and the mountain air gets colder and fresher as the car ascends to 7,000, then 8,000 feet. Soon the sky is a cloudless blue and the expanse of water shimmers in clear sunshine. I've heard songs about California since I was little; I've read about it and wondered about it and here we are at last.

We need to get out of the damn car, to walk and rest and breathe fresh air. It's a huge relief to leave the arid desert highway.

In Tahoe we have a "lakeside cabin" for four days—they call it a cabin but we call it a mansion. It's a five-bedroom, four-bathroom chalet-style palace next to the lake, with a wraparound wooden deck. At night we sit on the deck in shorts and thick sweaters and listen to the waves breaking on the shore. When it gets cold we go inside and light candles, cook dinner together: steak or pizza for Tom, vegetables for me, plus whole-wheat bagels. In the mornings, Tom gets up early and drives to Starbucks and comes back with triple-shot Americanos, while I slice fruit and burn toast. This is heaven, or at least the most beautiful place on Earth.

It was bright and cold in Denver and Boulder, snowstormy in Wyoming, and finally sunshine and warmth in Lake Tahoe—and I get to wear my new bikini. This is something of a departure from my usual black two-piece—it has tropical fruits and flowers in orange, pink, and green, splashed onto a halter-neck style, and Tom loves it. I know my shape is changing, or else why would this new bikini fit me? Although I don't feel "heavier" (as I'd feared), my clothes don't hang off me as they used to. My jeans are snugger around the thighs and bum, my arms a little less angular. I don't know what to feel about this—mostly I try not to think about it. I've always avoided looking at my body in the mirror anyway.

* * *

In San Francisco we're back in city mode: rushing through Chinatown, climbing the 210-foot-high Coit Tower, scaling the hilly streets, crossing the Golden Gate Bridge. We spend a day on Tom's Kerouac research: visiting the Beat writers' former hangouts in North Beach and browsing for hours in City Lights bookstore (where the old Beatster Lawrence Ferlinghetti is actually in the office upstairs, although we don't get to meet him). After a few hours in the Beat museum, we cross Kerouac Alley and drink cold beer in the Beat bar Vesuvio. I haven't drunk beer for years; I'm starting to relax, I realize: it tastes divine. This is the bar where

Allen Ginsberg first read *Howl* and where Dylan Thomas hung out; it's now full of aging hipsters who look like they spent too much time with Jack Kerouac (and Dean Moriarty and Sal Paradise) back in 1947.

We take a tour of Silicon Valley, thirty miles out of San Francisco in the miraculous microclimate of Palo Alto. It's blisteringly hot out here and the fog of the Bay Area seems a distant memory. We drift around the enormous Google campus, soaking up the general weirdness of the place: the signs for the free Google canteens and film nights for employees, health talks and motivational seminars, the famous red, blue, and green primary colors of the Google bikes (employees pedal to meetings in different buildings), everyone we see is surfing or messaging on the latest Google Android phones, munching on free candies or potato chips. "Never more than 100 feet from food" is a Google mantra, which makes Tom look at me and roll his eyes. I wonder where this comes from: is it simply an American obsession with snacking, do they believe that food helps fuel creativity, or what? I've been doing OK with eating on our trip, but mostly sticking to safe foods: not exactly super-sizing myself.

Farther out of town, the Facebook premises are a low-key affair. There's no sign of Mark Zuckerberg—despite being a billionaire he allegedly works in the open-plan office along with his staff—but we score some free bottles of Vitamin Water from the friendly receptionist. (Raspberry and Pomegranate flavor, delicious, ice cold.)

Back in San Francisco Tom and I walk along the waterfront and stop to watch the sea lions. In a café on the Embarcadero we track down more fat-free frozen yogurt and fall on it like hungry animals. We're worn out. The trip is coming to an end in a few days and I think we're both ready. We drive out to the westernmost point of the city, where there's nothing but the Pacific

Ocean stretching into the distance, endless. This is it, the end of the continent: we've run out of places to drive, there's literally no more road left. We stand on the cliff tops and stare at the Pacific, dazzling in the sunshine, and I wonder what Tom is thinking.

I'm thinking it's time to face things; it's time to go home. I'm so tired of living out of a suitcase and packing up hotel rooms and never being in London for more than a few days at a stretch. Tom and I are always moving, and suddenly I long to slow down. Is this about having a baby, this longing to put down roots? But again those impossible questions rise up: *Am I responsible enough to be a mother? Are we really ready to give up our freedom to become parents?*

Chapter 10

Right Here, Right Now

"While you're writing, you ain't living."
—Bob Dylan

There comes a point in all this when I have to say: enough is enough. The procrastination has to stop: the food avoidance has to stop. What am I waiting for, after all these years? All the words in the world are not going to "cure" me of this eating disorder. In fact they're just distractions from the hardest challenge of all, which is to put on weight. And that Bob Dylan line reminds me that while I'm writing, I ain't eating.

Of course I believe that telling my story matters: I believe that the process of documenting this recovery is helping me, that self-awareness is important, and that learning from one's own experiences is preferable to simply giving up. I want to challenge the stigma of mental illness and explore eating disorders from the inside. I'm writing this book because I genuinely think it will help me (and others) beat anorexia. But even while I'm being more honest than I've ever been, I'm still restricting my food, maintaining my anorexic habits, pretending it's OK.

The reality is that I'm never going to write myself healthy. Time slips away—months have gone by since I began working on this book—and I've gained and lost the same few pounds. I've been so caught up in writing about it, making pledges and resolutions, answering emails and drafting chapters, traveling with Tom and eating low-fat yogurts—where is the progress? As always, I've been "too busy to eat." And that's just another excuse.

This time it's going to be different. It's the start of the summer now and I've decided this is my new beginning. I'm making this promise afresh and I mean it: I'm going to start eating. This determination has been building for some time—not only the frustration, boredom, and stupidity of anorexia, but also the desire for a baby. How can I continue to write about recovery without showing tangible progress? There's only so long readers will sustain belief in someone who isn't getting anywhere . . .

And there's my relationship with Tom. How much longer can I go on putting him through this? How much more of my hunger-and-food anxiety can he stand? He wants a baby too, and his yearning to be a father matters as much as mine to be a mother.

It matters terribly to me that Tom wants to be a father. It keeps me awake at night, how I'm letting him down, how I'm holding us back, because all this is my fault; I'm the dysfunctional one. We've tried so many times to get to the root of all this, to sort out my head and talk through the fears. Often when we're traveling on a train or a plane, Tom will seize his pen and notebook as we're talking, and draw up yet another list of strategies for my recovery. Then we both sign it.

I've kept them all, here in the top drawer of my desk, kind of alternative love letters. They include the Eurostar Manifesto (May 2010); the Kenya Treaty (Oct 2010); the Zanzibar Resolution (Nov 2010); the Cape Town Contract (Dec 2010); the Paris Agreement (Jan 2011); the Denver Declaration and the Sacramento Accord (May 2011); and just last week, the Albanian Affidavit (June 2011).

An example of one of these documents is as follows, written in a Starbucks in Elko, Nevada, in May:

- Start today (4/5/11).
- You are not fat; you will never get fat.
- Eat for our baby.
- Eat three meals a day.
- *Enjoy* your food.
- Sleeping will be easier.
- Life will open up for us . . . in so many ways.
- No running, cut back on cycling, not too much swimming but . . .
- We *will* join the best gym in London, for after the baby's birth. That's a promise.
- Treat this like army drill or marathon training: eat properly. No choice!
- Stop thinking, worrying . . . just do it.
- It will get easier.
- I love you.

The exact wording varies, but they're all similar to this, supportive and funny and reassuring. Tom sometimes says, exasperated, "Why do you keep them, Em? Why don't you follow them?"

Recently I've begun to feel immensely guilty about all this; surely it's too much for anyone to stand. I wonder why he doesn't go and get himself a normal girlfriend. I have said to Tom, if he needs a break from me, I would entirely understand. This weekend, in the car, I even suggested a separation: say, three months, where I have to get myself better, and he can have time off from all my neuroses. He said no, immediately; he wouldn't even discuss it. But I can see the desperation in his eyes and I know what a strain it is, being with me. I've been dealing with it for over a decade but, really, this wasn't what Tom signed up for, was it?

I notice that I always write, "it's been over ten years," or "more than a decade," when I refer to anorexia. That's self-delusion. I remember I did the same thing when I smoked—oh, I've smoked for about five years—even when it was closer to ten. Enough of the lies cloaked in vagueness; it's been nearly fourteen years now, which you could call an emergency.

* * *

The feeling that I need to take action has been mounting, but this week three things specifically happened.

First: I was at my sister Katie's flat on Monday afternoon. Her best friend Carla, a former model, had been having one of her regular wardrobe de-junks and had dropped off a trash bag stuffed with designer clothes. Like my mother, my big sister is extremely slight—they are both barely five foot two—whereas I'm taller with a broader frame, around five foot six, like my little sister, Alice. We both wear size nine shoes, whereas Mum and Katie are size five.

Carla's designer cast-offs are usually too long for Katie, so she cherry-picks the pretty tops or shirts and then invites me to look through the rest: skirts, trousers, etc. On Monday, while she fed the children their supper—fish cakes with new potatoes—I tried on dresses and jeans, wandering between the kitchen and bedroom, alternately cuddling baby Theo (my nine-month-old nephew) and gossiping with Katie. The conversation went something like this, although we mouthed certain phrases to keep it clean for the curious four- and six-year-old ears of my nieces.

Me, zipping myself into a sequined cocktail dress: So, when you got pregnant the first time around, how did you know? Was there a moment before you did the test when you just woke up and felt different?

Katie: I don't know really . . . we were skiing that Christmas, and I remember not wanting any alcohol, which must have been a sign, and Charlie said I seemed really tired—just wanting to collapse and stay in every night, then we got home and my period didn't arrive. So I did a test.

Me: But were you actively trying for a baby? I mean, how long had you been trying for?

K: Well, we'd been married about a year I suppose . . . we agreed it would be nice to think about babies but we both assumed it would take ages. I'd come off the Pill in October, and then I guess I conceived sometime in December—so it was quite quick! But Em, that's a good sign—if your mum and sisters are fertile; it runs in families.

Me: I suppose. But Katie, it's exhausting, trying all the time! I'm so jealous of women who have regular periods, because at least they can do the charts and work out when they're ovulating, whereas I have no clue. Remember the doctor who told me it's possible to ovulate without having periods? I want to keep things spontaneous with Tom, but I also know we both need a break sometimes. I wish I had a definite fertile window each month, you know? I'm running out of ways to make it interesting . . .

By this point we're both laughing and the little girls start laughing along with us too.

K: I know—if you have three or five or ten days when you can go into action it's definitely less exhausting *[whispering]*—we haven't had daily sex for years! But listen, maybe you need to take a new perspective on this. You feel powerless because you don't know what's happening inside you: if you're ovulating, if you can conceive, right? There is something you can do. Forget the horizontal baby-dancing for the moment, that's not the problem here. What you *can* do is get to your target weight. We know there's nothing medically wrong, all you need to do is to bump up your calories and get your periods back. (She's smiling at me, encouraging, and I'm smiling back, baby Theo gurgling as I joggle him on my hip.) Em, it's empowering, it's exciting—you're in control—you can actually do something about this!

Katie's absolutely right: until I'm at my target weight, about 120 pounds, why am I worrying about conceiving? I haven't done the simplest (and hardest) thing yet. I'm still hovering around 110 pounds because I'm scared to move forward. Going from 108 to 110 pounds was a huge hurdle for me; going above 110 pounds seems almost unimaginable. But to hell with that. I need to gain the extra pounds—whatever it takes to start menstruating again—and then we'll see about babies.

Nine or ten pounds. I can do this.

And the clothes? I scored a black pair of Whistles trousers (my nieces told me they looked smart) and a white shirt from Gap (you can never have too many white shirts) and a fantastic pair of Rock and Republic jeans (two inches too long, but I've since taken a pair of scissors to them). So, a good haul of designer swag and some really good advice from Katie. As so many times before, she got me back on track.

* * *

The second thing was this: on Wednesday evening, after a midweek film date in Leicester Square, Tom and I were at his flat in Mortlake. We were in the kitchen; me chopping broccoli, Tom prepping his pizza to put in the oven (he adds extra ham and chili flakes and hot sauce). Apropos of nothing, Tom casually mentioned that he'd weighed himself and realized he'd put on more than nine pounds in the last month or so. Nine pounds?

Tom, opening the oven in a gush of hot air and prodding the melting cheese on top of his pizza: I know, weird isn't it? I was 128 pounds and now I'm 138, just like that. Dunno where it came from—probably all that American food—anyway, it's good news. I've always thought I should be 145 pounds, now I'm aiming for 155. Might even get some of those protein shakes to drink before the gym, actually.

Me: I can't believe you've put on nine pounds and it doesn't even show . . .

Like me, Tom is slim (I can wear his shirts, sweaters, even jeans), but the difference is that he eats for England. I honestly don't know where his food goes—hollow legs?—but he can pack away hamburgers, steaks, fries, sandwiches, chocolates, and cakes without it showing up on his frame. He's not skinny—he works out in the gym every lunchtime and has strong shoulders and arms—but he's wiry, muscular. He often says he should "bulk up" (men want to increase their size while women want to reduce it) but no amount of food seems to affect him. So this news that he's recently gained nine pounds is surprising.

More than that, it's massively encouraging. One of the main reasons I can't gain weight has been the fear that a few extra pounds will give me lardy thighs and ass; that I'll become wobbly and fleshy and excessive. Throughout this journey of recovery I've wanted certainty: that I won't get fat; that my eating won't spiral out of control; that my weight gain won't continue until I'm obese—but of course no one can give me that certainty. They can reassure me and encourage me, but no one can guarantee what will happen.

Tom's development is the closest thing to proof I've had: his weight gain doesn't even show! If the closest person to me can put on 9 pounds and I don't even notice—and nor did he—then surely, surely, I can do it too?

* * *

The third trigger was last night in a West Sussex hotel, when we finally watched the DVD of a short film I'd made back in April, just a few months ago.

We drove down on Friday to review a new hotel for Tom's column. We'd been given the Henry VIII Suite, which was like something out of a Tudor historical romance—all mahogany wood, burgundy velvet armchairs, hanging tapestries, and a four-poster bed. The bathroom was vast, with dove-gray marble floor tiles and an antique claw-foot bath.

It was one of those rare, idyllic weekends when everything comes together: the sun shone and we walked along the pebble beach and it was even warm enough, between breezy gusts, for a quick dip in the sea. In the spa they treated me to a body massage and ice facial while Tom met the hotel manager over lunch, getting the information he needed for his review (and a bottle of red wine under his belt).

Then, after another stroll along the beach and dinner, Tom went to the bar to fetch us two large glasses of sauvignon blanc. We flopped down on the red velvet chaise longue and slipped in the DVD.

After the anorexia column launched in *The Times*, I was contacted by a few TV producers about the possibility of making a documentary. I had some meetings and came to the decision quite early on that I didn't want to get involved with reality TV. As someone who was brought up without a television in the house—and has never owned a television—I've never understood the point of it. Nor was I willing to prance around in my underwear (skinny girl makes shocking viewing), nor could I cope with the idea of a camera following me around, nor was I ready to be filmed in a café being "unable" to eat a plate of fries. I don't need to be humiliated, publicly, to see how idiotic this illness is.

I'd sit through meetings and the producers would ask me personal questions and outline their ideas, using words like "hard-hitting" and "unflinching," and I'd nod and open up, then afterward I'd go and sit in a café and realize that I felt violated in some obscure way. Why let everyone peer into your problems, your family, your bathroom mirror? The things I was revealing to these strangers just seemed inappropriate and undignified: my absent periods, our attempts to conceive, my boyfriend's emotions. Writing about it is one thing, filming quite another.

I'm still in contact with a couple of the producers. They are both independent TV companies making interesting documentaries, but they seem to do it without resorting to sensationalism or fly-on-the-wall nosiness. I've explained the limits of what I'm willing to get involved in and they mostly seem to respect this. For once in my life it's nice to feel relaxed about failure or success; because I don't yearn to be on television, I don't particularly mind whether it happens or not.

I'm reminded of what Ernest Hemingway said: "A writer should write what he has to say and not speak it."

Anyway, we spent an afternoon making a showreel: explaining my reasons for writing the column, discussing angles for an investigative documentary with my own story as the backdrop. The producer asked lots of questions and two guys stood behind the cameras and it went fine; I didn't think much more about it. Then, a fortnight ago, they sent me a DVD. I felt a little curious: what had they made of all those hours of conversation?

I've heard it said that anorexics should see themselves on film, but never realized quite how powerful the experience would actually be. The final reel, edited down to fifteen minutes, opened with me standing in a park, blue jeans against a green canopy of leaves, uplifting music in the background and the letters of my name spinning across the screen. Then it cut back to me on their sofa, discussing my "journey" so far. The camera roamed around while I was talking (I didn't remember that), focusing on my thighs in blue denim, zooming in on my hands—they look massive on the end of scarecrow thin arms—my eyes filling with tears at one point, later laughing at something the producer says, all the while looking not like someone who is recovering but someone who isn't well at all.

Objectively speaking I suppose they did a good job—Tom said the film was "beautifully made"—but I won't ever watch it again. The truth is that whatever I feel inside my head, whatever I believe about my own gluttony, I am still very thin. I was shocked at the person on the screen: that's me. That's *me*. What have I done to myself?

When we finally dragged ourselves from the sofa over to the four-poster bed, Tom fell asleep instantly. I was too unsettled to sleep.

* * *

So that was the third thing that happened this week to make me determined to put on weight. This attempt is not like the others, where I reach 108 pounds, then panic and drop back down again. I want to recover, and this time I mean it.

Don't believe me? I'm typing this in the Reading Room of the British Library. Strictly speaking food is banned here, but I'm in a corner and it's quiet today. At home this morning, before cycling here, I had a pot of natural Greek yogurt and a banana. Since I got to the library I've eaten a whole bar of Marks & Spencer milk chocolate and three Brazil nuts. Perhaps that's a strange breakfast combination, but it's forbidden food, don't you see? Chocolate contains fat; Brazil nuts contain fat—they are the very epitome of my fear foods. To gain weight I need fat. To have a baby, my body needs fat. This is a major step forward.

I can't tell you how much I'd prefer to be sitting here chewing peppermint gum or swigging a Diet Coke, all hungry and sharp, instead of wallowing in nuts and chocolate. I can't explain why— maybe that's just anorexia—but I can taste the fatness on my tongue and I long to be clean and empty again. I'm not advocating or justifying that hungry feeling, just being honest.

* * *

I have to believe that I'm not greedy, that I do deserve to eat, that I'm not worthless or fat, that anorexia is just a temporary setback. I have to keep telling myself that it will get easier each time I eat. In the words of the best-selling book, I have to *feel the fear and do it anyway*.

Some of that self-help stuff is quite good, isn't it? I can't pretend I've ever found it particularly effective, but there's nothing like a self-indulgent, empowering, you-can-heal-your-life fest. This is what is currently taped to my kitchen cupboards:

- A picture of the Olympic athlete Jessica Ennis torn out of *The Sunday Telegraph* magazine looking strong, not skinny.
- A photograph of my nephew Theo sitting on the floor in Katie's house in France—he's about six months old, wearing a pair of tiny blue pajamas.
- An image ripped out of *Runner's World* magazine of a female athlete drinking a bottle of water and holding weights: a fantastic body, toned but muscular, not waif-like.
- A visualization which I'm supposed to repeat as I drink my morning coffee: "Imagine your ovaries ready to release a healthy egg. Allow yourself to heal; give your womb the nourishment it needs; give your unborn baby the chance to live . . ."

You get the general idea—I'm trying to surround myself with images of positive strength: women who are strong and sexy (not thin and weedy), affirmations to encourage PMA (positive mental attitude). And baby Theo is there to remind me just how much I want a child of my own.

Apart from the affirmations, what else am I doing? I'm confronting the "full" feeling as part of this process. When you starve yourself your stomach shrinks; that's a well-known fact. Therefore my stomach is rather small, so it's going to be uncomfortable eating more at first. This was never going to be pain-free. I've spent fourteen years getting into this mess, so I can't expect to undo all that damage instantly. I feel full as I sit here in the library. I hate feeling full, but if I'm going to make progress now I have to accept the sensation of fullness.

I'm not letting me bullshit myself anymore about food. What kind of bullshit? The chocolate debate is a good example. I used to love chocolate and have been considering eating a few squares before bed, maybe with a milky drink. It would be a relaxing way to wind down at the end of the day with my bedtime reading, eating a few chunks of delicious chocolate— lots of women do that in the evening, right? But then I started thinking about all the caffeine, and how it might stop me sleeping (a two-ounce piece of milk chocolate contains around 25 milligrams of caffeine, which is why insomniacs are advised to avoid chocolate as well as coffee before bed), and I decided I'd better not risk it: a classic dodge on my part. Instead, with this new-found determination, I thought, *To hell with it, I'll eat the chocolate in the morning.* It doesn't matter when, just get it in. Chocolate may be an unusual breakfast but it doesn't matter; the point now is to gain weight.

According to Tom, "fruit is not a meal." I'm struggling to get my head around this one—it's tricky when you're hard-wired to think that a banana equals breakfast and an apple equals lunch. No, apparently fruit doesn't count. He keeps saying I should have a whole-wheat roll with every meal, but I find yogurt or soup or beans much easier to eat than threatening, carbohydrate-heavy bread products. Liquidy things. Why is Tom so obsessed with bread and meat?

In a rash moment, probably brought on by the unaccustomed sugar rush in my bloodstream, I decide I should simply double the portions of everything I eat. Now that would be bold. Could I do it? I zip my laptop into my backpack and nip out to the piazza of the British Library, stopping to pick up my black decaf Americano at the Last Word Café. I find a quiet corner of the courtyard, away from the traffic noise of the Euston Road, and call my mother at home in Camden. I apologize for interrupting her morning's writing and update her on my milk chocolate achievement. (What is this? I'm thirty-three years old, and I'm acting like a child telling her mummy she ate up all her greens.) I ask what she thinks about the double-portions strategy. Mum is encouraging but a little skeptical, which is understandable, given my past form. She reminds me that "the quicker you put the weight back on, the less painful it will be." She's right; I need to act fast.

But this is only the beginning. Right now I feel giddy, even manic—I'm eating chocolate and feeling super brave. The fat and sugar in my veins are making me wild, hungry, I want more and more, chocolate and sex and sunshine; I want to fast-forward this recovery. I'm so relieved to be making a fresh start. And yet, there's plenty of struggle ahead. The worst is when your clothes get tight—I know this because I remember it from the last time around. When I went from 77 to 98 pounds back in 2001, I felt like I was dropping off a pair of Gap Kids jeans at my local thrift store every week. And so, even as I consume the morning's chocolate ration (trying to ignore the shrieking taunts of "greedy" in my head), I'm anxious about the weight gain to come.

Chapter 11

Just a Tsunami Inside . . .

I've always been volatile, but over the recent months of early summer I've noticed that the emotional extremes have been getting worse. If it were simply the elation of the high times and the despair of the low times I could deal with it, but it's more than that. Of late I've had episodes of violent aggression, moments of such intense rage that I might do anything: attack someone, jump off a cliff, smash a glass into my face, open the car door and leap out while Tom is driving at ninety miles an hour on the freeway.

Last week, a van driver cut me off on Marylebone Road, then braked sharply at the red lights nearly causing me to crash into the back of him. When I drew up alongside and gave him the finger, he shouted out of the window that "f*cking cyclists should get off the f*cking road" and I was a "stupid c*nt in need of a good f*ck." Without a second's hesitation I got off my bike, strode over to his window, and punched the door frame so hard that I still can't bend my little finger.

When this anger comes upon me, it's like a switch has been flipped inside my brain; there's no rational cell left in my body, everything is on fire and I can't even think for the red storm that is fogging up my synapses. I fling the pot of yogurt across the kitchen, hurl the dinner plate out of the window, throw my bike down in the middle of the Euston Road and threaten a van driver. The rage is uncontrollable and I simply don't care about the action or its consequence. It's like a hyperkinetic explosion in my brain. I know these episodes are dangerous; I know I could hurt myself or get into serious trouble. I don't know what's happening sometimes. I don't know myself.

In desperation last week, I emailed my friend Deanne. We first met around six months ago when, in response to *The Times* column, she wrote offering help. She explained that she was not only a professional eating disorders counselor, but also a mindfulness practitioner. I was skeptical at first—the concept of mindfulness has always seemed slightly flaky to me—but agreed to meet. Deanne isn't flaky but she is incredibly calm and thoughtful, a soothing presence to be around. We sat for hours over coffee in the Royal Society of Medicine talking about our lives, and have stayed close ever since.

Emma, stop for a moment. Take a deep breath. You sound so anxious. I understand about this anger. I would lay a bet that you aren't becoming a nasty person, but these feelings are really scary. I don't think you will ever know your nature until you have harnessed the energy in the anorexia to work for you; to trust you will be OK and human, with facets like a diamond. Sometimes these facets look dark if the light is behind you, while the same facet will shine if the light passes through.

Deanne tends to communicate in these wafty terms: "harnessing energy" and "shining like a diamond." At first it made me roll my eyes, dismissive, impatient; I wanted practical solutions, not new-age abstractions. It was only when I concentrated on what she was actually saying that it began to make sense.

Anger is like a huge room; what you see of it depends on which window you happen to look through. From one window you can see that your rage is a consequence of change in anorexia: when you've bottled up your feelings for so many years they erupt like a volcano.

What's wrong with you? Just a tsunami, Em . . . there must have been an earthquake underneath, so wait and see where the earth settles.

I agree with you that blame is useless; I agree there comes a point when we have to stop blaming anorexia, or our own shortcomings, or past relationships, or fear. The tsunami inside asks to be heard; to be faced, perhaps, and then you will be able to see it for what it is . . . You are on a really wobbly step right now, but I promise there are many other steps ahead. Perhaps consider letting someone help you leap to the next one.

* * *

What was *wrong* with me? "Just a tsunami . . . wait and see where the earth settles." What beautiful words.

I hope Deanne is right. I hope it's the process of recovery that is causing this instability. The surge of energy—from eating—seems to fuel all sorts of unexpected emotions. After so many years of anorexic numbness I find myself coming back to life in a whirlwind of feelings. And I feel like I've failed in some way, that the eating disorder has beaten me. I know I'm angrier and more impulsive than before; is this just the earthquake doing its thing? Sometimes I simply feel angry at the whole world—for making me confront this, for making me leave the anorexia behind. It's part of me. I feel defeated.

And yet—it's more than just extra caloric energy and awakened feelings. For too long, everything that's gone wrong in my life has been blamed on anorexia. Even when Greg killed himself, I don't think there was space for bereavement, not properly. Everyone was on the alert for my weight to plummet, for me to plunge back down toward 85 pounds; no one ever thought of what I'd already lost. Greg's suicide had nothing to do with anorexia. I am so tired of hearing that everything would be fine if I just ate more.

What if it goes deeper than that? Of course eating again has set off the volcano, of course my emotions are bubbling over, but I refuse to accept that it's always about food. I believe there may be an underlying chemical imbalance, something wrong with my brain, spinning me on these rapid cycles from violent rage to numb despair. My inner chaos has always been more real and troubling to me than the eating disorder, but no one takes it seriously. Like Tom, they insist I will feel calmer when I start to eat regularly.

Until a few years ago I didn't know what it was called . . . I still remember the lightbulb moment when I read a description on the Internet of cyclothymia.

Cyclothymia is known as a "milder cousin" of bipolar disorder. Like bipolar, cyclothymia's distinctive feature is its mood swings from high to low, although they tend to be less extreme than those of bipolar disorder. When you're up—or hypomanic— you feel confident, energetic, omnipotent: anything is possible. There's an exhilaration about everyday life; you could be a kite, soaring way above the Earth. In my upbeat phases I need hardly any sleep or food, I'm full of ideas and plans, creative, productive and talkative, giddy with joy. But when you're down, you feel useless: pessimistic, clumsy, and depressed. It's hard to concentrate and hard to look forward with any hope: the future seems bleak. Physically, you swing from intense periods of activity to lethargic periods of paralyzing depression. The mood fluctuations with cyclothymia can be unpredictable: sometimes I feel quite stable for weeks, sometimes I cycle between severe highs and lows in a single day.

Have you ever read about a condition or an illness and felt instantly, *Yes, that's it*? When I began to find out about cyclothymia it spoke to something that had been niggling at me for years. In some ways it's a relief to have a label—an unofficial label—for my inner chaos.

Does mental illness run in families? We don't talk about it, but there is a lot of psychological instability on the Woolf side of my family. Sometimes I wonder how my father has coped at all: both his parents committed suicide, both his sisters suffered repeated nervous breakdowns (as have many of our cousins and extended family), and my little sister has experienced serious episodes of depression. So my instability is part of me. Is it part of my family? And if it's definitely genetic, a neurological condition rather than my own general messed-up-ness, should I still be taking something to control it?

I took Prozac for seven years and I still miss it. I'd love to be able to pop that neat green-and-white pill every morning. It makes you feel good—I often long to return to the speedy, zippy high of those Prozac years—although I barely slept and never stopped moving and was even more hyperactive than normal. But, since 2002 and Greg's suicide, I don't entirely trust chemicals.

It's not that I "disapprove" of drugs; this is a personal, not a moral decision. I know mental illness is real: I know something in the brain has gone badly wrong. I know the right medication really does save lives. Prozac was a miracle for me. It worked its mysterious magic on my serotonin when I was at my thinnest. For a while at Oxford, I was so precarious that I could barely make rational decisions. My parents believe that Prozac rescued me when I might easily have gone on slipping down, into hospital and then death. But I have decided to deal with my own imbalances without chemicals. It may not be the right decision—it's hell sometimes—but I want to live with the emotions and experiences as I'm feeling them. I want to do it alone. I want to learn to "deal with" life, raw. Back then I couldn't have coped without Prozac, but I can mostly cope without it now.

Depression or cyclothymia or anorexia. A toxic mix, the three torments, all exacerbating each other. Whatever the science says, the stigma remains. I'm ashamed of my dysfunctional brain. I hate how demanding I am, emotionally, mentally. I need to talk and talk, euphoric, veering on manic. Then I fall silent, I stare down at my large stupid hands on the end of skinny arms. When Tom asks me what's wrong, I can't put it into words. I'm unable to go on, overwhelmed by the hopelessness of it all, crushed by my own sense of failure. No one understands. My family says I'm erratic. I wear myself out with the highs and then I crash and I suck all the air out of the room with my lows.

But I don't know how to be stable. Is something broken inside my head? Am I going mad? I was never the world's best sleeper, but the insomnia has gotten a lot worse over the last decade.

It was 5 AM and starting to get light when I got back from a night ride this morning, twenty miles through the deserted streets of London. Since I gave up running the muscles in my legs ache and twitch painfully; my entire body misses the endorphin rush. Cycling isn't quite as good, but it's better than lying in bed awake. I cycle for hours and then I stand under the shower feeling empty and clean, but still not sleepy. I would give anything to sleep.

My little brother and I were discussing sleep last week in the pub. He does circus trapeze and walks the high wire; he thinks sleep is all a state of mind. I told him about my insomnia. He looked at me for a moment, his head on one side, and said,

"Actually yeah, I can't imagine you sleeping ever. You're kind of too intense." I feel desperate because it's true, I don't know how to turn off. I wonder if I slept as a baby.

For me, trying to describe the experience of insomnia would be like trying to explain the pain and loneliness of severe migraine: I can't find the words. You spend hours staring into the dark while the rest of the world slumbers; you go from hope to frustration to rage to despair. There's nothing you can usefully do at 3 AM and, anyway, you're exhausted. You would like to be asleep.

At night I lie next to Tom and watch him sleeping. I wonder what he's doing right and I'm doing wrong. He lies face up, on his back, like a corpse. He can sleep when there's light or noise, even when he's stressed: he has learned how to lie down and switch off. Sleep deprivation takes you beyond reason, it makes you irrational, sends you mad; that's why it's an established form of torture. Sometimes I wake Tom up and he strokes my hair and turns my pillow, gives me a massage with lavender oil. We talk for hours, making plans and working out problems, and the darkness seems a little less endless.

And now I have added insomnia clinic to the list of appointments: acupuncture, yoga, mindfulness. If I could learn to sleep I think everything else would fall into place: I would be calmer, life would be less of a battle, I would be rational about food. But it's all or nothing with me, it's always been that way. Either I have rigid control or everything is wildly out of control; there seems to be no middle way. I can't sleep because I can't unwind; I can't start eating because I might not be able to stop. If I'm not skinny, surely I'll be obese. It's so tiring, the internal conflict and the guilt and the endless fight: isn't it time for a ceasefire?

There's nothing cool about being this screwed up. And poor Tom. It's wearing us both out, this unpredictable soaring and plunging from happy to wretched, empty to full. At the heart of it all is the desperate longing for balance. But if the chemicals in my brain have gone haywire, how will I find equilibrium?

* * *

Mental illness is not easy to experience, nor is it easy to be around. So when I suggested to Tom that he take a break from me, I was absolutely sincere. It wasn't something that just popped into my head on the freeway; I'd been thinking about it for weeks. This is a conflict of my own making and I don't have any choice but to fight—but Tom does. The strain it's putting on him makes me hateful to myself. I didn't fall in love with Tom when I first met him; it's been incremental falling over these past two years. It surprises me now, how precious he is to me, how it hurts me to hurt him like this.

Sometimes I'm overwhelmed by Tom's kindness: I've never felt I deserved to be so loved by anyone. I don't mean romantic declarations or grand gestures either; I mean the little things he does on a daily basis, without reminder, without reward. Whenever we go away, for example, he packs his pair of soft blue tracksuit bottoms that I love because he wants me to be cozy. Even though I normally put on a bathrobe after my evening shower, still there have been cold bedrooms, or hotels without bathrobes, or the heating doesn't work, and he can't bear me being chilly or uncomfortable. Every single trip, even if we don't need them, he always makes sure to bring the navy tracksuit bottoms; then he takes them home and washes them, remembering to use fabric softener. This is why he keeps asking me to move into his flat; because he wants to look after me, he wants us to be together all the time, not just when we're traveling.

I remember a recent evening in Edinburgh, a bitterly cold Easter weekend. After an eight-hour drive from London we arrived at the hotel, checked in, and were shown up to the fourth-floor "Da Vinci suite." It would have made a stunning art gallery, but it was unwelcoming as a bedroom, sterile in the way that high-concept interior design often is. And it was frigid, the trendy exposed radiator far too minimalist to heat even a quarter of the cavernous space. Tom disappeared while I was running a bath—I assumed he'd gone downstairs to ask for an extra blanket. It turned out he'd walked from the hotel into town in the pouring rain, and spent £80 on a cashmere sweater for me from the only shop still open. I hadn't complained about the chill—I could improvise with a couple of tops, and I wouldn't have wanted him to go out into the rain—it was my own fault for not packing enough warm clothes. But he dashed out anyway, and returned half an hour later with this elegant ribboned Whistles bag (containing the softest sweater I've ever owned) and a bunch of white lilies. "For being lovely, Em. For always coming with me to endless hotels, even when we just want to stay at home . . ."

He didn't want thanks, he just wanted me to be warm.

* * *

Remember how my mother and I joke that I'll never find the perfect man because she's already found him? Like my father, Tom seems to have an endless capacity for giving, a bottomless well of love. After renewing my pledge that I will eat more—after eating my chocolate in the library as I promised—I get an email from him. It's around 10 PM and I'm reading in bed (*Jude the Obscure*) when the red light on my Blackberry flashes.

*Em-love—hope you're OK and getting an early night—
fantastic weekend but tiring. Avoided traffic jams driving back
from yours, crashed out on sofa and watched Chelsea lose, then
I wrote up action plan for you, as threatened. The plan takes
us to the last Sunday in July, when I've booked us tickets to see
The Cherry Orchard at the National Theatre. Seemed like a nice
way to celebrate! I'll list the main principles—and put simply,
after so much talk, and so many manifestos, this is the one that
has to come true. This is the real deal. Don't wince when you
read this: it has to happen now, or the summer will disappear,
no progress will be made, and that would be incredibly sad.*

Action Plan—a.k.a. The Six Weeks That Changed My Life

- *As agreed, you will eat three meals a day. Each meal must be
  a proper, balanced meal.*
- *A proper breakfast consists of a large bowl of muesli with
  milk, fruit, handful of Brazil nuts, vitamin pills. Alternatively
  it could be toast with jam, fruit, nuts, and vitamins. It must
  include carbohydrates of some sort. On no account can
  "breakfast" be a piece of fruit and low-fat yogurt (see below).
  The word "breakfast" involves the breaking of a fast, not the
  continuing of a fast.*
- *A proper lunch consists of a cheese sandwich with a piece
  of fruit on the side. Alternatively a baked potato with beans.
  Or a pot of couscous with a roll, or vegetable soup with roll.
  Note: it must include carbohydrates and some protein in the
  form of beans or cheese, etc.*
- *A proper dinner might be vegetable chili with baked potato,
  grated cheese, and a side salad, or it might be a vegetable
  curry with brown rice and a salad. Or pasta arrabbiata with
  cheese sprinkled on top, or vegetable lasagne, both with*

salads on the side. You need to branch out and try different dinners that include proteins and carbohydrates.

- *You must keep a food diary covering the three meals a day (I don't want to hear your usual objections to this). Be it as simple as "breakfast: muesli, lunch: cheese sandwich, dinner: baked potato and veg chili." This way you can, quite crucially, keep tabs on what you are eating, making slip-ups impossible.*
- *At the end of each week, we'll assess the week gone by. There must be no gaps. No missed meals whatsoever.*
- *Low-fat yogurts and fruit do not count as meals.*
- *Steamed broccoli and a roll does not count as dinner.*
- *There must be no buying of "low-fat" items: those items are for people on a diet.*
- *No resumption of running (but remember the best gym in London).*
- *All of this starts now.*

I believe that after six weeks of a new diet your body will be much healthier, the sense of well-being and happiness will pass into your subconscious, and your body will send messages to your brain that "this is good" and "I rather like this." Until you were nineteen you never had difficulties with food: you enjoyed it! By being systematic, never cutting out a meal, and never pretending that certain food counts when it blatantly doesn't, these six weeks can provide the jolt that is required. Don't think about anorexia. Those attitudes have to go in your personal trash can. Just follow the program and see what happens. It's like watering a neglected plant, remember?

I hate to be so forthright, but really this is it. Everything that can come from this is positive. I believe that we should do this together: how else is a child made? And I promise you a new writing desk, if you want to move in properly and commit to living together. Remember sitting by the river in Dresden, last summer, discussing the future? Imagine, we can sit by the Thames before The Cherry Orchard *at the end of July and things could be so different. You can do this xx*

Chapter 12
An Inconvenient Truth

Three weeks on, it's June, and I've been making limited progress with Tom's action plan. It should be so simple: "just follow the program and see what happens"; "let the system take the strain and thought process out of it." It sounds logical—appealingly, deceptively easy. But if it were that simple to take the thinking out of eating, anorexia wouldn't exist. Without wanting to minimize Tom's generous, thoughtful attempts to help, all his patience and support, I nonetheless know he'll never have an anorexic mindset. He's trying to understand what I'm going through and find a solution, but he's not trapped inside it. It's at times like this, confronted with a simple "action plan," that I realize how powerless anorexia makes me. If you've seen someone with anorexia confronted with food, you'll know. Tom knows. It's humiliating.

I know this explanation is no explanation at all; this is at the heart of the struggle, because it's so hard to untangle, because an eating disorder really doesn't make sense. It's not that I can't see the beauty of a six-week action plan; it's not that I don't want to recover, enjoy nice meals, and improve my health. So why not just follow the plan? This is the mental illness itself. This is what anorexia is.

But I'm trying so hard. I've been gradually weaning myself back onto whole-wheat bread and rolls (although not at every meal). I have issues with hot food—especially at lunchtime—and

I prefer to stick to cold food throughout the day. I'm still avoiding cheese, although I remember that when I had to gain weight after Oxford daily cheese sandwiches were a useful building block, and I'm frustrated that my cheese phobia has returned. Chocolate doesn't bother me quite as much; why should one fattening food be more acceptable than another, I wonder—what constitutes a "fear food"? I know anorexics who would struggle to put a piece of chocolate in their mouths. For others it's bread, or pasta, or any carbohydrates at all; for me it's cheese (and butter and margarine).

All the while, I have to not think about gaining weight or acknowledge this physical process. I try not to register the reality of what is happening to me. I throw out tight jeans, telling myself not to mind (although of course I do). I rejoice in the resurgence of my breasts but wince at the size of my thighs if I catch an unfortunate glimpse in the mirror. There is still no sign of my periods, and this is starting to really get me down. Not menstruating for all those years never made me feel like less of a woman, but it's starting to now. My face has a few spots—*Is this a good sign*, I wonder, *are my hormones finally waking up?*

(*Stop thinking about it; stop analyzing every spot and twinge and mood . . . Just carry on, eat the goddamn Kit Kat, ignore the voice, keep eating.*)

This may sound exaggerated but for me the whole of June has felt like a white-knuckle ride: I am gritting my teeth, steeling myself for the expansion of my body that I know has to happen. I am a sky diver willing myself to be brave; I am a rock climber, clinging on by my fingernails.

Inevitably, there are good days and bad. I have moments when I'm full of energy, when I know I can do this, strong and determined. My hair looks shinier, even my fingernails are stronger. I try not to panic about getting fat; I try not to despair about my chances of getting pregnant. Always, always, there's the constant concern about the extra pounds.

* * *

"But where will it go?" I repeat, trying to keep the panic out of my voice. My big sister and I had planned to go and visit an art gallery but we're curled up on her sofa instead. "Five whole kilograms—that's over ten pounds—where will it go?"

I can see Katie's trying to keep a straight face and I know how ridiculous I sound. "That's the same as five bags of sugar—just imagine, saddlebags of fat hanging off my thighs and backside . . . I'm sorry, but that's a lot of lard to be hauling around on my bum!" We're laughing so hard now that Katie swallows a mouthful of doughnut the wrong way—quite impressive given that she's also breast-feeding her baby and balancing a mug of tea in her free hand. I can't tell whether it's the idea of my expanding bum or if she's really choking, but it feels good to laugh.

"But where will it go?" This is a major preoccupation for a recovering anorexic and something I used to ask my psychiatrist all the time. Fortunately Dr. Robinson had the patience of a saint. He was used to the anorexic's endless need for reassurance in the face of body confusion. He would explain again, "The weight will go on all over. I can't pretend it's going to be uniformly even, but you won't gain ten pounds just on your thighs. Weight gain is made up of fluid, bone, and muscle; there's just slightly more of you. Everything weighs more, your liver, kidney, even your brain." I find this oddly reassuring: I like the idea of my brain and internal organs getting larger. (Say what you like, but no woman wants an extra ten pounds of fat on her bottom.)

Anyone who thinks gaining weight will cure anorexia is wrong, wrong, wrong. The body confusion continues.

* * *

It's now early July and my editor at *The Times* asked me to "update the readers" on my weight. I hate weighing myself and I don't own a scale. In the column I have been purposefully vague about weight gain, because it doesn't help me and I know it won't help other sufferers (anorexics are great ones for comparison: who is lighter than they are, who eats less, who looks skinnier, who wears smaller-size jeans). And, just like a photograph, printing your exact weight is guaranteed to elicit one of two reactions, especially from other women: "Oh my God, she's still way too thin," or "So what's the big deal—I weigh less than that—why is she calling herself anorexic?"

But if it's what my editor wants, I can hardly refuse. This is the point of the column after all. I'm aware that I am on trial, in some very public way (a trial perhaps of my own making, but uncomfortable nonetheless). I'm aware that I need to show physical, as well as psychological, progress. I understand that I've entered into a pact with readers—they follow my story and I try my best to provide the happy ending.

So this morning I force myself to climb onto the scale in Tom's bathroom and unscrew my eyes to stare at the digital display . . . 114, 113; it flashes and sticks on 114. OMG—114 pounds.

Tom steps out of the shower and sees me standing on the scale. Fortunately he's blind as a bat without his glasses, so he can't see the numbers. "All OK, Em?" he says, cautiously, reaching past me for a towel. Well, what else can he say? He knows that if my weight goes down I'll be depressed and if it goes up I'll panic.

But now the scale tells me the truth: at some point in the past few summer months I have tipped over and above the magic weight of 110 pounds. Say it: *I weigh nearly 115 pounds.* So I'm past the danger point, over the barbed wire, through the psychological barrier of 110 pounds. Of course this is the point of my personal challenge—this is the point of all the chocolate and bread rolls and Brazil nuts—but it's frightening progress. Do I feel relieved? No, I feel huge. This is the highest weight I've been since I was nineteen years old; my BMI is now at the low end of "normal." It's a shock, after so many years of being in the "underweight" zone on the BMI charts, to be leaving that behind.

You may be thinking, 110 pounds sounds fine. You could weigh even less than I do and be perfectly healthy—fertile and menstruating. But I've wasted years telling myself that my weight was fine for my height, and it's not: the body doesn't lie. And I'm still not cured. I may be heavier, but I'm no less screwed-up about food.

* * *

In addition to the recent surges of anger, I've been experiencing powerful waves of another long-lost sensation: hunger. This is the inconvenient truth: the more you eat, the hungrier you get. After years of perfecting the art of emptiness, now that I've started to eat, I find I'm hungry all the time. I don't mean peckish, the way you might feel if you missed lunch—I mean ravenous. Sometimes I feel so hungry I think I'll burst into tears or go mad. I've been trying to read but I can barely concentrate on the words in front of me. I keep wondering whether I should just give in and eat.

It's not just my body that's hungry, it's like my mind has gone haywire—I never felt this nuts when I was starving myself properly. I really am off the scale. This isn't like "I could polish off an entire package of cookies," or "I could murder a pizza with all the toppings" . . . My new appetite is bottomless; it's like I could eat the whole world. I feel as though I could suddenly spin out of control. Having lived for so long with one simple rule—don't eat—it's frightening to break that rule. This is the closest I can get to explaining the fear that all anorexics feel: fear of change, fear of losing control, fear of recovering and finding that real life can't be governed by one simple rule. And anyway, what if I start eating whenever I'm hungry and then I find I can't stop?

None of that matters. All that fear is just me finding excuses to dodge food, and ruin a brilliant relationship, and hide behind *what ifs*, and waste my thirties the same way I wasted my twenties. I've always known that putting anorexia behind me would be the hardest thing I've ever done—and so it is. All I can do is hold on tight. For too long I've been waiting for something to happen, something to kick-start my eating, but nothing's going to happen if I don't make it. For now I am holding my nerve.

So here I sit on a midsummer morning in London, calm in my corner of the British Library, writing about recovery and knowing that I'm finally on the road. Yes, I'm gaining weight. But the constant hunger unsettles me. Why, three hours after the self-inflicted breakfast chocolate, do I need to eat again? Is this normal? How often does hunger strike? I leave the library and wander five minutes down the road to the shiny new St. Pancras station. Crowds of tourists mill around, talking, laughing, and eating. I skulk around Marks & Spencer, bewildered by the raging hunger inside me.

Food makes almost zero sense to me. Everything seems so complicated. I stare at the shelves and try to focus on what I'm hungry for. *Listen to your body*, isn't that what they say? But what could possibly assuage this ravenousness: an egg and watercress sandwich, a jar of pesto, a packet of salt and vinegar potato chips? I feel like a mass murderer, stalking the aisles, greedy, restless. I don't eat chips, obviously. Pasta salad?

I end up in the fruit and vegetable section, my old familiar hunting ground. I buy an apple for lunch, and grapes for a snack later, and leave the shop with my grumbling stomach. Maybe I should have bought the sandwich, but eggs have been problematic for me for years (surely they're just unfertilized chicks and therefore not really vegetarian). And anyway, every sandwich or salad I've inspected seems to be drowning in mayonnaise—and possibly butter too. What is this yawning gulf inside me?

I'm aware of the contradictions here, of course. I say my stomach has shrunk and that's why I get uncomfortably full, and yet I'm claiming to have an insatiable hunger? This is the paradox of anorexia: the emaciated body, the fat mind, and the greedy, empty stomach. I can't promise to give you a coherent narrative; I can only promise that it's authentic. Everything is mixed up, and something as simple—some might say pleasurable—as food becomes fraught with danger. Meals are a time of intense mental conflict for me.

A few months ago, while writing an article on mothers with anorexia and its effect on their babies, I came across a research study from the seventies. "It has been argued that people with eating disorders have particular difficulty in distinguishing somatic sensations, such as hunger, from emotional feelings such as affection and anger" (Bruch, Hilde, *Eating Disorders: Obesity, Anorexia Nervosa, and the Person Within*, 1973, Basic Books: New York). At the moment, this is honestly how it feels—my hunger is unsettling and upsetting. Before I could just ignore it (I can handle the fiercest of empty-stomach pains), but now I'm supposed to respond to it. So I prowl my kitchen at night, opening and closing the fridge and cupboards; I haunt the supermarkets —unable to put my finger on what it is I need to eat.

Walking back to the British Library eating my apple (lamely awarding myself a gold star for eating in public), I realize that feeding myself is impossible. Look at me—I don't even know where to start. Of course this is what Tom's "action plan" was designed for: to take the angst out of recovery, to provide simple rules for me to follow. But it's not working—even the simplest meal plan is a threat. And this is why they call anorexia the "deadliest of mental illnesses"; this is why the mortality rate is so high and the recovery rate so low. Because we feel that feeding ourselves is "giving in."

I sit down at my corner desk in the reading room, still hungry. Balzac isn't going well. I can't take in the words on the page in front of me, let alone translate them into English. How did I get from that positive upbeat conversation with my mum, when I vowed to eat double portions (and put the weight on quickly), to this experience of utter supermarket paralysis? Why is this process so jerky; why do I keep lurching from determination to helplessness?

I find an old notebook from years back, from one of Dr. Robinson's clinics, I think. Scribbled along the margin are the numbers 101.2, 101.6, 103.6, and 102.5, which I take to be my weight. (God, I was tiny then.) As I flip through the pages it all comes back and I can hear Dr. Robinson's voice, explaining again how the first stage of recovery is usually pretty difficult—he's seen it in hundreds of recovering anorexics, no one can predict how the weight will go on; there's no way to control it, just that the process is different for every patient. "Fluid retention, uneven fat distribution, and replenishing glycogen stores in liver = probable weight fluctuations." He'd tell me things can take months to settle down, but eventually they will. "The rapid rate of weight gain will slowly drop off, metabolism will continue to increase—and more food will be needed to gain weight later." Rereading this now, I can't work out whether I feel better or worse.

* * *

In theory, I understand what's happening here: a little food stimulates the appetite. Eat nothing at all and your stomach gives up hope. My natural appetite has kicked back in, simple as that. I suppose I should rejoice that the machine—my appetite and hopefully my metabolism—is grinding back into action. But this is what I feared all along, that I'm greedy, needy, and insatiable. It's the thin end of the wedge, isn't it? Relax the rules, start eating food regularly, and your appetite rages out of control. To be honest, starvation was easier.

This is another reason why anorexia is such a hard nut to crack. Think of other addictions, alcohol or drugs, and it's all about *not doing*. If you can just avoid the addictive substance, that's a start. Avoidance, abstinence—these are concepts I understand. Denying my urges, going cold turkey, not allowing myself things are what I'm good at. But there's no simple roadmap to quitting anorexia: as I've said before, it's about starting something, not stopping. Hard as I found giving up smoking (and I did), I just exerted every inch of my willpower during those first few days of powerful nicotine cravings. I was determined not to give in. I remember how proud I felt, beating an addiction that (as we ex-smokers like to remind everyone) is "stronger than heroin." But, it turns out, beating anorexia is infinitely harder. You're surrounded by food all the time, but the "greedy" voice in your head is as loud as ever. You can't avoid eating altogether—no one can—but it's the one thing you can't handle.

How does anyone handle food without spiraling out of control into gluttony and obesity? How do other people eat? In all these months of discussing it with close friends and family, I don't think I've ever really asked. I decide to do what I keep being told to do (*reach out, ask for help*) and ask those close to me how I should deal with this hunger thing. I put down Balzac, fire up my laptop, and start typing emails.

The first reply comes from my aunt Alison—my mum's younger sister. She and my uncle Keith now live in Bridgnorth, up near Wales, so I don't see her that often, but we were close when I was a child and we've recently rediscovered each other.

You're hungry? This is excellent news, well done, Em! I'm delighted to hear that you're noticing what your body is telling you. Of course you're ravenous; you aren't eating enough so your brain is sending you messages. Remember learning to swim? Or to ride a bike? It's scary, and you're not sure you're doing it right—and sometimes you don't and hurt yourself and have to pick yourself up and start again—but there's a point when you just have to take the plunge. That's what you've done; that's why you're terrified. All those thoughts that have kept you trapped all these years won't disappear overnight, but I promise you, if you can just hang on in there and use all the loving support you've got around you, then you'll beat them. Focus on people who love you and will support you—like Tom and Katie and me, and no doubt lots of others too. We won't let you fall.

It's really difficult to give any practical advice when I don't know what or how much you're eating now, or how you feel about particular foods. I imagine your stomach will be easily upset if you aren't used to eating much, plus all the stress you're under. I'd maybe think about bland, comfort food, definitely some carbohydrates, which is what generally works for me when I'm really hungry. Do you ever have porridge? It's my great comfort food—granddad used to leave a big pan of it on the stove for us on winter mornings, and funnily enough Keith has started making it recently on our Rayburn! What about good-quality bread— nothing too heavy, maybe something with unbleached white flour. Toast is my other comfort food, and soup! I think the best advice though is to eat what you feel like and you can worry about all the health stuff later. Honestly, a few months of eating an unbalanced diet really isn't a problem. Just practice staying afloat before you worry about technique.

I think long and hard about porridge, toast, and the alien concept of "comfort" food. I vow to practice staying afloat before I worry about technique. Then I get an email from Sunray in Switzerland, my friend from the BBC Health message board. I suppose it's that odd Internet mix of anonymity and intimacy that have enabled us to be honest with each other from the start: me about food, Sunray about fertility. She's just had two babies in quick succession, both boys, after years of trying. Like her online pseudonym, Sunray is full of optimism; I don't think I've ever once heard her beaten.

As silly as this advice may sound, if you're hungry the only answer is to eat! You're still underweight; your period still hasn't come back. You can't think about "getting fat" at this stage. You have to think about "getting healthy," and there's a big range of "healthy" before you get anywhere near fat.

Protein foods are fantastic for filling you up and they're healthy. Brazil nuts are a fabulous way to stop the hunger pains. But, girl, you've got to eat more than 2–3 nuts, okay? Cheese is another treasure food, as is peanut butter. The idea might make you shudder, but now that your body's learning to be properly hungry (not starving hungry, but healthy hungry); you need to encourage that.

I can imagine it's frightening to "give in" to your hunger but you have to realize this is how to beat the anorexia, and it gets you another step closer to the baby you want.

You ask what normal people eat? I concentrate on three big meals a day, plus 2–3 snacks: a huge bowl of cornflakes and linseeds, rice cakes (about 6–7), an apple, a tomato mozzarella sandwich (big enough that it doesn't easily fit in the mouth, LOL!), corn cakes, some handfuls of mixed nuts, and then a full dinner plate—and I often go for seconds! That amount of food just covers my needs and keeps me full of energy for the boys. Each person is different but that's the sort of quantity you need to be a healthy weight with kids.

A few things to consider when you're pregnant:

—The lighter you are, the more weight you need to gain to make sure you and the baby stay healthy. If you were overweight, you could afford to gain a little weight, but being underweight, you'll need to go over the top when pregnant and eat loads! To give an indication, when I was pregnant first time I gained nearly five stone (70 pounds)—yes, you read that right! TBH, I loved putting on the weight, and had a great time pigging out! I was of the opinion of making the most of it and I'm glad I did ;-) That meant that, after giving birth, I had plenty of fat reserves to supply me with desperately needed energy.

—I hope this isn't the case, but you need to be prepared for morning sickness. I was lucky that my morning sickness was mild so I ate as normal. But, unfortunately, many women do suffer from it and lose weight in the first trimester because they're so poorly. You need to have enough fat that you can cope with any morning sickness that might come.

So, how can you eat like a normal person? The only way is to stop food controlling your life. Food is there to enjoy, not get stressed over. At this point in time you need to think about quantity and quality (lots of fats and proteins!). Please don't worry about "getting fat"—at the moment, it's impossible for you. Take care my dear.

I also email my little sister, Alice. She isn't the first person I usually turn to, not because I don't value her advice, but because she has enough health issues of her own to cope with. In Alice's case, the issue is ME or myalgic encephalomyelitis—also known as chronic fatigue syndrome. She's had it for years now, since she left university. At first the symptoms were fairly mild—like bad flu—and she was able to live a normal life. After graduating she moved to Italy, went through a series of handsome Italian boyfriends, and had various jobs in Rome and London. However, over the last five years the ME has become much more severe. For everyone in the family, it's a mystery: not that we don't want to help, but that we don't know how to. There's still no medical consensus on what ME actually is—a virus, a person's autoimmune system attacking itself, a psychological condition—and no cure. Just as anorexia makes those around me feel powerless to help, I feel the same about Alice and ME. I wish there were something I could do.

In many ways, Al and I are the closest of us children—we're the nearest in age (just twenty months apart) and similar in so many ways. Whenever I hear her voice on a phone message I think it's me talking, and we have the same tastes in clothes and makeup (and the same bad-frizzy-hair days). We spent all our time together as teenagers, juggling dates and wild nights out, and we're both much quieter now but still up for the occasional cocktail. We have similar thought processes: I can tell how Al will react to a situation instinctively. Like many close siblings, when we're communicating with each other, we hardly need to finish our sentences.

Al emails back when I ask her how she deals with hunger.

Hey Em, it sounds to me like your natural appetite which has been suppressed for so long has kicked back in, which is healthy and normal. As you know with the medication I experience a lot of hunger, but I just try to eat plenty of lean protein, vegetables, pasta and oats and things like that. Three proper meals a day is a good place to start with healthy fats like avocados and lovely salads with vinaigrettes. Maybe write a meal plan of some sort? Babe I know you're worried about not being able to stop but if you allow your body to "guide" you it will tell you how much to eat. It's about making friends with yourself, I think, instead of this self-punishment thing. You will not get fat overnight. Remember, it takes years of overeating to put on weight. Try to feed yourself with love and care and that might help with the fear you're feeling. It is possible to put on a bit of weight without getting out of control!

It makes me feel very lucky to have all this help—and yet helpless, and humiliated. A significant part of my anorexia for more than a decade has been about rejecting the outside world and being independent, not needing other people or their food. What an irony, now, to be reduced to this, asking for guidance on such a simple matter. I need constant reassurance that it's going to be OK. I am pathetic. I am like a small child.

And recovery is so erratic. I veer from barriers up to floodgates down; I clam up and then I fall apart. I want to follow everyone's advice; I want to believe Tom when he tells me, "It's just part of the process, Em. In a few months this stage will be behind you and you'll feel strong again. Keep eating, things will work out." I don't feel strong, I feel weak. I read everyone's advice and I try to put it into practice. I have to believe that a balance will come naturally, that I won't always feel this out of control. But the lion-hunger inside me continues to roar. I don't even know what I'm hungry for. Maybe, just maybe, it's nothing to do with food at all.

Chapter 13
Thank You

Long before Tom and I met I had made attempts to recover from anorexia—attempts that always fell by the wayside. My next promotion, or training for a half-marathon, or an ex-boyfriend, or a new bathroom seemed more important at the time. I didn't really want to get better, so anything was a convenient distraction. And I was full of fear: if I managed to gain three pounds I would panic and lose five. But now it's different. Now I see that getting better matters, that life with an eating disorder isn't a full life, that health and babies and love are important. I'm starting to learn that battling oneself every day isn't necessary—and that maybe, one day, cake might be a pleasure.

But I didn't understand any of that until I met Tom. I simply didn't believe I could recover. Anorexia was (and still is) the most powerful force in my life, but before Tom I didn't have a strong enough reason to take it on. So Tom, thank you:

- For the hundreds of breakfast trays you've carried up to hotel rooms to spoil me, those elegantly sliced fruit platters and silver coffee pots (when I know you'd prefer to stuff down a bacon sandwich, skip your shower, and hit the road).

- For presenting me with a set of proper Moleskine notebooks, like yours but in a range of rainbow colors. It made me feel like a bona fide journalist—and the very next day I got my first commission from *Harper's Bazaar*.

- For not minding my spoon fetish: for accepting all the small silver spoons that have turned up in your kitchen drawer since we met, even though they don't go with the rest of your cutlery set.

- For the way you astonish me by sometimes eating bacon and sausages at breakfast, chicken and/or turkey at lunch, and steak at dinner. That's a lot of animals in a single day . . .

- For going around the corner to Sainsbury's to buy Slimline Tonic for me on rainy evenings when I've given up alcohol again (even though we both know you have an ulterior motive—to pick up another bottle of wine).

- For sending me postcards from every town you visit—Slough and Coventry and the other dodgy trips I didn't come on (my mailman thinks I'm really weird)—and for doggedly writing those daily updates on the weather, the mad landlady, what you've had for dinner.

- For that night in St. Moritz when you called the hotel's room service for mint tea and then had a mini-midlife crisis: "What am I doing? How did it come to this? I'm nearly forty years old, sipping mint tea in a bathrobe!" and we both nearly died laughing.

- For putting aside *Stella, Style,* and *You* magazines plus all the review sections for me from your extensive Sunday newspaper delivery every week without fail.

- For the study you've created for me across the hallway from yours—for clearing out your golf clubs and cricket paraphernalia and transforming it into a writer's room (although the green baize card table from your parents wobbles when I write).

- For the promise of our trip to Hell Bay, for the promise of a real writing desk, for the promise of a daybed . . . a girl's got to have something to look forward to, right?

- For your sense of entitlement—those ludicrous statements such as: "This bedroom is the size of a cupboard, I shall need an upgrade; I went to see my parents and they only served me a chicken pie; I would have gotten into Oxford but the interviewer didn't like me . . ."

- For getting your shirts professionally laundered and ironed at the dry cleaners around the corner. I tell you it's a waste of money but I'm secretly glad you'll never ask me to do it.

- For all the plane rides together, for helping me survive the agonizing long-haul flights (or just drinking enough red wine to knock yourself out), and for those three days on the tarmac with "engine failure" in Chicago, Newfoundland, Boston, and finally London . . .

- For always packing the soft tracksuit bottoms and candles and massage oil, for making me cozy wherever we go, for caring if I'm warm, for running around Aberystwyth trying to find decent hair conditioner.

- For understanding my thing about hygiene and for (mostly) taking a shower every day when I'm with you, for accepting that I need multiple showers/baths daily, for washing your hands after you've come back from work on the tube and before you hug me, for understanding that I have to wash my hands frequently in public places.

- Further, for changing into clean "flat jeans" so as not to transmit the dirt from the London Underground onto the sofa, bed, or chairs.

- For pretending to be pleased with the electric toothbrush I gave you last Christmas out of concern for your dental health, for sometimes even using exfoliating face wash.

- For running me a deep bath—at the right temperature and with the best, the only, Ren Moroccan Rose Otto bath oil, every time I'm close to losing it.

- For putting up with my frizzy-hair days and not reacting when I laugh at yours—should two people with such terrible hair really be allowed to procreate?

- For (just about) coping with my insane need for privacy and independence and my horror of being someone's property; obviously I'm awful at this business of relying on others, but I'm learning.

- For the jewelry:

  - The diamond earrings from Antwerp (you'd barely dropped me off at the train station before you were having a run-in with the shop owner).

  - The amethyst-drop earrings from Windhoek, that fortnight when we broke up and you sobbed your way around Namibia in an open-topped jeep, sending tear-stained letters from the desert and incoherent emails while I sat at my office desk and tried to hold it together.

  - The Tiffany silver "bean" necklace (or is it a tear-drop?) that you gave me on our anniversary in Barbados in a real Tiffany box and turquoise bag with white ribbons.

- Best of all, the green emeralds from Colombia, which flash in my ears like tiny rocks and which you negotiated in a back-room deal with shady local characters.

- For coming to Leonard Cohen concerts with me all over the globe, and for loving his music almost as much as I do . . . we've only listened to *The Essential Leonard Cohen* what, 5,000 times?

- For rescuing me from the bathroom in Krakow when I slipped and cracked open my chin, for calling the ambulance, for those hours in the waiting room while I sat in the emergency room, for gripping my hand really tight while the Polish doctor sewed me up *without an anesthetic.*

- For not shouting at me for leaving oil and tire marks on your pristine hallway. It's impossible to carry a bike up those stairs without touching the walls, but I will repaint them, I promise.

- For not minding that I woke you up last night (and most nights when I can't sleep), for holding me and telling me rubbish stories, for the plans we've hatched and the books we've devised and the journeys we've plotted in those sleepless hours from 2–5 AM, for all the night talking; thank you, Tom.

Chapter 14

An Ovary Scan and a Moving Van

It's the first day of August, the day of the scan. I've waited months for this appointment and I'm hoping for good news. The last time I had this scan, nearly three years ago, there was no indication of any dominant follicles. In other words, the eggs were not maturing, so the ovaries weren't releasing eggs; hence no menstruation or conception. Although I haven't completely ruled out taking the fertility drug Clomiphene, I know that natural weight gain is the safest route to getting my periods back.

The scan—the "transabdominal and transvaginal ultrasound," to give its full name—is the only certain way to see what's going on in the reproductive system. After my efforts at gaining weight, today feels like the moment of truth: I alternate between hope and pessimism. In optimistic moods I tell myself that of course I'm making progress: I've been eating healthy, nourishing food, and I've cut back on the exercise; it's all good. My body is resilient, it will respond and recover; everything will happen just as nature intended. I even allow myself to daydream a little, usually when cycling around town: what if I'm already fertile but just don't realize it; what if I've already conceived? I remember what the experts have told me—that it is possible to get pregnant without having periods. But for every positive thought there are many more negatives. I'm like a stuck record sometimes, saying to my mum, to Tom, "But why is nothing happening?"

My worries are enough to fill an ocean and more. What if the extra pounds have no effect whatsoever—could anorexia have left me permanently damaged? It's the kind of story you see in *Heat* magazine all the time: "crash-dieting made me infertile"— unscientific, sensationalist, but alarming. What if my ovaries have gone to sleep forever? To be honest, I don't have a plan B at this stage; Tom and I have never discussed adoption or egg donation or surrogacy. It's way too early for that. Right now, all our hopes are focused on the scan.

I don't tell anyone, not even Tom, how tense I am about this. If I were religious I suppose I'd be on my knees, but instead I just worry and hope and then worry some more. Last week, in a panic, I emailed Dr. Robinson, and received this reassuringly scientific response.

Your body will work when it detects enough fat: that can be at a BMI of 19, 21, or even 23. Usually it happens around BMI 22. Regarding ultrasound scans, there are three stages. Stage 1: ovaries are small and little is visible within them. Stage 2: multi-follicular stage; ovaries are larger and full of roughly equal small-sized cysts, around 5 mm in diameter. Stage 3: the dominant follicle where one follicle grows much larger than the others, around 16–18 mm across, is often associated with ovulation if weight and nutrition are maintained. Fourteen days after ovulation a period occurs (unless you become pregnant). Therefore, the further you are along the stages, the more likely you are to ovulate.

So far, so good; it all sounds perfectly logical. Except, as Dr. Robinson always reminds me, things are never that simple.

The closer you get to a healthy BMI, the more likely you are to ovulate . . . However, the relationship between weight and ovulation is not 100 percent—the body is never black and white. The scan might be reassuring, but it's just as likely to show that you need to put on some more weight.

More weight? How can I put on more weight?

The last lines of his email tell me what I want to know—and what I've asked him so many times before—but each time, it keeps me going:

You can be reassured that in the majority of women with anorexia nervosa who have recovered, the system recovers and fertility is normal. One further point, the ultrasonographer might comment on the lining of your uterus, which is very thin in anorexia and gets thicker as you put on weight . . .

It's miraculous and infuriating and rather magical, the way the human machine calibrates itself. All those invisible calculations and transactions between cells—too little body fat and hormone levels plummet, eggs don't ripen, the uterus thins. When you're starving the womb becomes an inhospitable place for a baby, with good reason. And yet everything else carries on—the heart pumps, the lungs breathe, and the brain stumbles along; so many complex systems interacting to keep the essential parts of the machine functioning, even when you're not bothering with food or care or rest.

If I ever get to the end of this drought I will never take a period for granted again.

* * *

So, the long-awaited scan. It's a Wednesday afternoon, one of those uncertain late summer days, when sudden sunshine gives way to thundery showers almost hour by hour, the lead-gray London skies broken up with weird shafts of sunlight. I meet Tom outside Belsize Park tube station and we walk up to the Royal Free Hospital. It feels strange to be back in the place where I came for my appointments in the Eating Disorders Unit. The hospital has recently had a million-dollar refurbishment so it looks different, but it still stirs vivid memories of the misery and coldness of those eight years. I don't say anything to Tom as we walk past the sign: ADULT PSYCHIATRY, THIRD FLOOR.

In the spotless new reception room (full of pregnant women) we hold hands and chat lightly about work, the weather, the weekend, but not about the scan. I don't really know what we're talking about because my stomach is knotted up with nerves. Only a few minutes after my allotted time, a sonographer appears at the front desk and calls my name. Tom squeezes my hand, and I go through to the imaging suite with her.

There's a brief exchange about why I'm here, my medical history, and then she asks me to undress and lie down on the couch. The procedure isn't exactly pleasant, but it's not painful either: similar to a pap smear but with a tiny camera instead of a speculum. I remember what an ex-boyfriend, a medical student at Barts, once told me: "Never feel embarrassed by having an internal. Doctors have to examine all sorts, homeless people who haven't washed or who have urinated on themselves; for a doctor it's routine—they don't worry and neither should you." Remembering that advice always makes me laugh. And today, in the imaging suite, I don't care about the discomfort or indignity involved; I'm just desperate to know what's going on inside.

I should point out that, despite having counted down the days until the scan, I wasn't expecting immediate results. I assumed the sonographer would do her investigations and capture the relevant images and then just send a report to my GP like last time. But this middle-aged woman, wearing a hijab over her white coat, is quite chatty and forthcoming. Given my unfortunate position on the couch she seems amused by my precise questions, but she's happy to answer them. Will she be able to tell me if I've ovulated? No. Would she be able to see if I was pregnant? Yes. Please can she measure everything carefully? Yes. When will my GP get the full results? Seven to ten days.

There's a swirl of black-and-white images on the screen above the bed. "OK . . ." She focuses on the images. I hold my breath. "Good. So what we're seeing is normal, exactly what I see every day of the week; everything looks healthy." Am I hearing things? I ask her to repeat what she's just said. "Yes, it all looks completely normal." I realize I'm fighting down tears—first relief, then excitement—as I listen to her steady voice and gaze up at the screen.

Moving the camera around inside me, she presses down lightly on my stomach. Then she points out the black dots: these are the eggs that are ready to be released. "See, Miss Woolf, in the left and right ovaries, plenty of dominant follicles. And the uterus lining is very good; I can't see any problems here." She smiles at me. "I can't say anything about trying for a baby, but structurally, this is all perfect." I'm speechless; I think I'm going to burst with happiness. When I ask about my absent periods, she suggests two things: one, gaining a little more weight might well trigger them, or two, taking Clomiphene.

We talk for a while longer, and she tells me she'll write up the report for my doctor as quickly as possible. I pull my jeans on and practically dance back to the waiting room. Tom is engrossed in the sports section of *The Times* and looks surprised to see me, having expected the whole process to take much longer. "How did it go?" he asks, looking concerned, but I can't speak. Instead

I drag him by the hand, through the revolving doors and out to the parking lot, to tell him the amazing news: that everything's normal, there are lots of eggs there, it's game on.

It's raining heavily now but I don't even notice because we're hugging so tight. If I ever had any doubts about us having a baby, Tom's smile is my answer. We finally calm down and start walking toward the tube, holding hands and talking about the future. My God, it's no wonder that women get so emotional about their twelve-week scan—I'm not even pregnant yet and I'm in pieces. This feels like a new beginning.

* * *

We go back to Tom's flat and he announces he's making us a celebration dinner. I put on my new sea-green dress and light candles and open a bottle of champagne, while Tom does his chef thing—making a mess of the kitchen, contentedly "slaving over a hot stove," swigging glasses of red wine. Tom calls me his Puerto Rican dancing girl (we bought this dress in San Juan a few weeks ago) because it swirls around me, fluid as silk, every time I move.

The starter is an arugula, spinach, and watercress salad with a garlicky olive oil and balsamic dressing; my mum taught me to make this dressing, really simple and delicious. The main course is a spicy chili (vegetarian for me and meat for him) with brown rice. I never realized Tom could cook because I've never really given him the chance, but the chili looks and smells amazing. At first my taste buds are overwhelmed by all the complex flavors—and of course I'm worried about the oil in the salad dressing, the size of my portion, the hidden, dangerous, mysterious ingredients. But Tom reminds me that kidney beans and rice are excellent sources of protein and iron. And, despite my anxiety, it's nice to share a meal that has been cooked with love.

Apart from the salad dressing, my culinary contribution to the evening is dessert: fresh strawberries, raspberries, and blueberries topped with vanilla frozen yogurt. It reminds us of our U.S. trip back in May, sharing tubs of frozen yogurt in Salt Lake City. After, we take our champagne through to the living room and play Leonard Cohen on the iPod. Curled up on the sofa together, my feet propped in Tom's lap, we reminisce about the road trip, all the miles we covered and places we visited.

Thinking back to the spring, I realize how far I've come: I couldn't have eaten Tom's vegetarian chili back then. Not only have I gained weight, but I also have a more varied repertoire—after years of sticking to the same fat-free, safe options. For anyone else who is trapped with anorexia, let me say this: for all the fear—and it's a hugely fearful process for me still—it's also exhilarating to take responsibility for your health. When you're not panicking, there are moments of actual empowerment: you're taking control of something that has controlled you for so long. Because anorexia is tyranny, that's all.

I remember something Tom said to me, months ago. We were in Bruges, warming up in the café of an elegant patisserie in the midst of a heavy snowstorm. All around us people were eating plates of hot buttered toast, slabs of Belgian chocolate, wedges of cheesecake. At a corner table by the fire, I remember Tom's words, " . . . but fat doesn't make you fat, Em."

It's the strangest thing to discover: that eating fat doesn't make you fat, that a vegetarian chili won't make you gain weight. There are no rules. You can experiment with flavors; you can explore the unknown. Daring to taste something new doesn't mean you're greedy or a failure. You can feed your body when it's hungry (though I still struggle with this one). The anorexic mindset is relentlessly black and white: things are either safe or unsafe, good or bad, thin or fat; I know this, I think like this. But it doesn't have to be this polarized. I drizzled oil on my salad. I ate Tom's chili. For longer than I can remember my life has been all or nothing; now I'm starting to discover shades of happiness in between.

Shades of happiness like packing the dishwasher together at night, sharing the last sips of champagne, getting ready for bed. I lie awake for hours, smiling, replaying those black images on the screen, those dominant follicles, any one of which could contain the ingredients of a baby. I'm normal—yes, *normal* normal. For once that sounds just perfect.

* * *

"But I don't understand—you're not living together?" My aunt looks confused. "Are you planning to move in with him, or waiting to get pregnant first, or are you going to have this baby on your own?" We're drinking coffee in Covent Garden and the conversation has taken an uncomfortable turn. Alison is asking what I know a lot of people are wondering about us: *If they don't even live together, how the hell are they planning on raising a child together?*

The scan was a breakthrough of sorts, but talking to my aunt reminds me of another element of "recovery" that I have yet to face. The primary goal I set myself, all those months ago, was to gain weight: to challenge my food fears and relinquish my rigid controls over eating. But there was something else in that pledge, not unrelated to the eating disorder, but in some ways even more difficult for me to face: "This year I'm going to kick down my barriers and let Tom love me and take more risks. It's time to let go." Yes, it's time to let go. Time to risk my own emotions, to learn to live in the real world, to open up to other people, to allow myself to take part. The scan, the real possibility of having a baby together, and then my conversation with my aunt, brings this sharply into focus. I've been putting it off for months, but it's time to move in with Tom.

Why is this such a big deal? For years I've watched from the sidelines as friends and colleagues move in with their "other halves"—sometimes successfully, sometimes not, but they give it a go. Apparently it's normal for human beings to seek life partners and to cohabit. We are social animals, naturally designed to gather in pairs or family units, to live together.

After years of therapy, reading, and weekends alone just thinking, I've come to understand more about why I've been isolating myself. It's simple: I got hurt and so I withdrew. First the breakup with Laurence, then Greg's suicide—different forms of abandonment but abandonment nonetheless. I had gotten too close to the flames and they burned me badly. Rather than risk further rejection it seemed safer to be self-sufficient. Nothing much can damage you if you don't really care. So in my twenties I reinvented myself: by way of isolation and anorexia, I became detached from things. I had plenty of boyfriends but I didn't fall in love again: when it came to emotional involvement, I'd put up barriers. Living alone was a part of this fortress mentality; my flat became my sanctuary.

Then along came Tom. It's inconvenient, falling in love and wanting a baby, when you're a confirmed one-person household. It means that I have to rejoin the outside world.

I remember when Dr. Robinson first suggested anorexia might represent something more than just an eating disorder for me; something deeper, some need for purity and control. I'd confessed an element of distaste for flesh-and-blood femaleness, the voluptuousness of pregnancy, the unpredictability of childbirth and motherhood. My private world, my pristine flat, my runner's body—all controllable, contained, and neat. I think Dr. Robinson has a point. Over the last seven years I've watched my big sister go from single career girl to married mother-of-three, and the chaos is unbelievable. Mostly it's happy chaos, I can see that—she and Charlie are fantastic parents—but it frightens me too. When Katie brings the children around they wreck my flat: they jump up and down on the bed and leave footprints all over my cream duvet and pull everything out of the kitchen cupboards and splash orange soda on the kitchen counters and leave bits of regurgitated food behind the sofa and traces of milk and baby puke on my white shirt. It's havoc. What about my freshly painted walls and gleaming wooden floors, the simple salad and crisp glass of white wine, the early morning swim? When I think of babies, it threatens my ordered life.

And yet, for Tom, it means everything that we should live together and start a family. So why haven't I moved in; what is my resistance about? It's about everything I've described above—the chaos, the compromise of communal living (even the word "communal" makes me shudder), the fear that it might all go wrong. My friend Jules, who is currently three months pregnant, emailed me last week. *I really think you should give it a try with Tom—making a home together is one of the loveliest feelings in the world. I remember when Nick and I first moved in; I used to delight in washing his dirty pants! That soon faded, but the thrill of living together never does. Now, the best thing about going away is coming back to him and our home together. I know you worry about losing your independence, but there are ways to have your personal space in Tom's flat.*

I think it's more than just a question of "personal space." I actually crave being alone. I guard my privacy as if the barbarians were at the gates. I find being with other people for extended periods of time exceedingly stressful. I like silence and order. I like my flat to be cool and empty. I have nothing on the walls (except a few photographs in simple silver frames) and I don't like people lolling on my sofa or sharing my bed. I don't like comings and goings, or washing-up in the sink, or piles of drying laundry. I don't like strange food in the fridge.

There's a paradox here, because Tom isn't the slobby, messy, male stereotype—far from it. He would never leave dirty clothes on the floor or unwashed plates in the kitchen. His bathrooms are spotless, the garden is neat. And I love his flat—it's spacious, airy, filled with sunlight. Like me, he's addicted to books, music and films. He has beautiful art on the walls and his flat is big enough for two (even three). More than that, he understands what a home needs to be. The way I feel about my flat—my refuge from the big bad world—is exactly what Tom longs to provide for me. He doesn't want all-night parties or endless house guests either. We both love nothing more than closing the front door, putting on a warm sweater and "flat jeans" (i.e. clean jeans not worn on public transport) and pottering around in privacy.

My only practical objection to Tom's flat is that it's in South-West London, eleven miles from where I grew up, but it's an idyllic setting, green and leafy, nestled in a bend of the river Thames. A few months after we met, Tom (secretly) converted his spare room, where he used to keep golf clubs and sports clutter, into a study for me with fresh white paint, a new wooden floor, and installed bookshelves. I didn't find out about it for ages—I never went in that room—but I remember the day he showed me the transformation . . . I stood in the doorway of "my" new study, sunshine streaming in the windows, genuinely lost for words. It was one of the most romantic gestures I've ever known, because it was done *for me*. That's Tom all over: dogged, generous, imaginative—showing his commitment to my writing through wood and paint. Creating a place in his home for me to follow my dreams. So why, two years on, have I still not moved in?

It comes back to the same thing—fear. The longer you live alone, the more private you become. Like gaining weight, it has become unimaginable for me to live with someone else. Giving up anorexia and moving in with Tom are inextricably linked. Since we met he has asked me to move in with him almost on a weekly basis. I remember an evening in Vienna, walking back to our hotel, when he said, "From very early on I've had this instinct to bring you near me and to look after you. I want us to create a world together." I used to find it seriously threatening, this notion of being looked after; now I find it comforting.

And yet I'm still hesitating. Tom has been getting increasingly upset by the "part-time" nature of our relationship, by the weekday evenings spent apart, by what he perceives as my lack of commitment. Although we probably spend more time together than many couples with all the traveling, it's not the same as sharing a home. It's taken me ages but I'm starting to understand this, that my reluctance to move in with him feels to Tom like rejection.

* * *

How did I get so stuck in this solitary way of living? I grew up surrounded by people in the most chaotic circumstances imaginable. I think back to my childhood—that noisy, loving family of seven—and wonder where I've gone wrong. But now, more than ever, is a time for courage. If I want to move forward, if I want to have a home and a child with Tom, I must get myself unstuck. I must change.

Starting the column and then writing this book have been life-changing experiences. Never did I think I'd leave a secure career in publishing to strike out on my own. Never did I think I could say the word "anorexia" out loud. Never would I have thought it possible to confess that I am addicted to starving myself, that I get high from the hunger, that my greatest fear was to get fat. Never would I have considered sharing these fears with a boyfriend. Or putting my trust in someone again. Never would I admit that my periods had stopped and if that bothered me, or that I am overwhelmed with anxiety about the future. Never did I think I could eat a piece of cheese or a bar of chocolate again.

I achieved it all. I survived it all.

Please don't laugh. I know the chocolate and cheese seem tiny, ridiculous, but they are huge triumphs in the face of anorexia. Call it narcissism, neurosis, the dieter's disease; whatever you call it, it's been the hardest fight of my life. And every triumph, however minor, brings a new strength, a spark of power, a sense of achievement (mixed with terror)—above all, a knowledge deep within myself that I can do it. Every time I challenge the fear, every time I do something impossible, the fear gets a little weaker.

* * *

And so to the next challenge: to move in with Tom. From independence to cohabitation, from "me" to "us." According to him, unless I move in we have no future. Maybe he's right. Of course he's right. And we want to be parents. My deep-down, unscientific instinct tells me that my body won't conceive until we're settled, actually living together. Making a baby takes two.

Lying in bed one morning I say, "Tom, there's something I want to ask you." My voice comes out all shaky. He turns his head, rests it on the edge of my pillow, and looks concerned. "What is it?" I take a deep breath. "If you still want—if you'd still like me to . . . shall I move in?" His face breaks into a massive smile.

We book a moving van for the last three-day weekend in August. I can't lie: I. Am. Petrified. But like most of our fears when we face them, the anticipation may be worse than the reality. Who knows, it might even be fun.

Chapter 15
Healing

Exactly ten months ago I wrote about setting myself this goal:

"—the biggest challenge of my life . . . over the next year I'm going to overcome anorexia . . . I'm going to reach a healthy weight so that I'm fertile again. (I'm not going to freak out when my period returns, I'm going to celebrate.)"

This morning I woke up and felt that low-down ache in my abdomen. I went to the bathroom and yes, my period's here. The hard work has been worthwhile. At long last my body is working the way it should, despite my best efforts to wreck it, despite the years of stupidity. I sit for a while on the chilly bathroom floor, overwhelmed with relief—and gratitude and respect for whatever's going on inside.

For years I've felt like a broken piece of machinery. Now I feel whole again. I've waited so long for the little red flag that will signal the start of new things. Finally it's here and I'm not remotely freaking out. It's the right time at last, I'm ready.

So many times over the past decade I have imagined this moment. Whatever I said, no matter how much I promised my parents, doctors, and therapists that I wanted to beat anorexia, that I wanted to be healthy again, deep down a part of me wanted to remain sick. I needed to be visibly thin; in some strange way I needed the chaos inside my head to show on the outside. Much as I fought for my independence and pushed others away, the anorexia—that most visible sign of falling apart—was the proof that I was struggling. I thought I was so strong and I looked so weak.

So I'm all mended now? Well, no, not quite. If you were to give me a plate of buttered toast for breakfast, or porridge with sugar and cream, there is no way I could eat that. Not even a mouthful. But I have, in my own odd ways (via yogurt and broccoli and raspberries and muesli), made sufficient progress to get to this point. Things are starting to happen. My period is back; my body has begun to heal.

What surprises me most is how happy I feel: not scared, not fat, just excited. I feel (cue cheesy music) womanly!

It's only 6 AM but I'm wide awake. I run a warm bath with rose oil and soak for a long time. If you asked me how much I weigh right now, I couldn't tell you and I don't care. Imagine that: *I don't care*. Right now, a whole new set of possibilities has opened up to me, and I can almost believe I'm stronger than anorexia . . . Of course this is a temporary euphoria (the anxiety will be back soon enough), but I'm so unused to this feeling of peace, contentment. All the fretting over scans and weight charts is irrelevant now: my body—with this small event this morning—tells me all I need to know.

I wrap a towel around me, go upstairs, and slide back into bed, fresh and clean. Tom turns, opens his eyes sleepily, and smiles. "All OK, Em?"

Yes. All OK. All very OK.

* * *

Last week's period was the physical marker of the end (or perhaps the beginning of the end) of anorexia, but the psychological recovery is still a work in progress. As I predicted, the anxiety has begun to creep back in, but I'm aware of it. I have the upper hand this time. I know what I'm feeling—"your period has come back, therefore you must be fat"—but I know it's not true. I understand where this anxiety comes from, and I'm trying to look it firmly in the face.

And here's the difference between this recovery and all my previous failed attempts: I didn't panic when my period arrived. I didn't immediately stop eating. I haven't changed my mind; I don't want to lose the weight again. There is so much chaos inside my head, I admit, so much to work through over the coming months. But I don't feel defined by the sickness anymore. I remember how I felt at the hospital last month when the sonographer told me everything was "normal." I really want to be normal now! Not fat, not thin—just healthy and active and OK. OK about food, OK about myself, OK about being loved.

That's why this is a story of love and recovery. Not that falling in love was the answer—there have been many ups and downs, and we're not out of the woods yet. Not that Tom cured me: no one can do that for an anorexic. As much as he and others have supported me, the hardest work was mine; when I say that every bite has been "agony," it's true. But it's been a gradual process of growing up, understanding my demons, letting the painful past fade a little, and finding someone with whom I want to live and love and have a baby.

Dr. Robinson always tells me "the body is never black and white." Well, neither is life. Not black and white, but a series of compromises, moments of black despair, moments of pure, perfect white, and lots of little flashes of color in between. In the end, loving someone else fully, which I couldn't do while in the grip of anorexia, was more important to me. Giving up control is frightening beyond belief, but there are compensations.

I won't lie: the pressures have been immense. Many of us know what trying to get pregnant can do to a relationship. One minute you're a carefree couple, enjoying each other's company; then you begin to feel that having a baby together would make things even better. In itself that's a romantic decision—I remember the emotions I felt when Tom and I first talked about starting a family—but it changes the agenda. Romantic sex becomes baby-making sex (or as the women on Mumsnet call it, SWI: Shagging With Intent), and inevitably the pressure builds. It doesn't have to ruin everything—you can still keep things spontaneous—but the dynamic changes. At best, deciding to try for a baby is a thrilling, intimate venture, but at worst it can become soul-destroyingly routine.

And of course when there are problems conceiving it's the "problem" partner who feels responsible, even though Tom reassures me that's not the case with us. At times I've felt like a total failure: no periods, barren ovaries, I'm inadequate. I've been holding us back, letting us down.

Then there's the age thing. At thirty-three I'm not in the last-chance saloon, but it's hard to ignore the dire warnings all around: how female fertility "plummets" in your midthirties, how modern women are "leaving it too late." Many friends have told me I don't need to worry for years yet; women are having babies later than ever these days. Female fertility is thought to be heritable and the signs in our family are good—my mother had five children, my big sister already has three, and neither of them had any problems conceiving. I'm not panicking yet—well, I'm trying not to—but I think about it a lot. The truth is, time goes really quickly. As one (male) reader unhelpfully reminded me, "your thirties are no time to mess around."

On top of the efforts to conceive and the ticking of the biological clock is the pressure I've imposed upon myself: of beating anorexia in public, of sharing the journey, and within a specific time frame. It's what that psychologist meant when she emailed months ago: *"I have concerns about this sort of 'reality' journalism in terms of the pressure it places on the individual in the public gaze."* I suppose I've been conducting an experiment on myself, and I'm OK with that. The exposure has been a mixed blessing: it has given me a purpose and a structure, a reason beyond myself for getting better. Whenever I've felt "greedy" for eating, or tempted to lose weight, it has enabled me to say, *No, Emma, you're doing this for a reason. You've made this public commitment and you have to follow through.* But it's also been difficult, at times, to keep writing about it.

The vast majority of responses have been kind, funny, supportive. I've received excellent advice, and I've met all sorts of strangers with whom I'm still in e-contact. Many anorexics have written to say that I've inspired them to recover too, and it's an unexpectedly lovely feeling for me to be helping others.

So why is it the harsh criticisms that stick with me? Why do I still remember the woman who called me a "narcissist," the man who said "get over yourself," the angry message that reminded me people are dying from cancer and starvation and I should stop being selfish and help others? Last week I received an email that informed me I was simply not ready to have a baby, that I'd never be a mother, and "God help my children" if I did. That message hurt me more deeply than I can say. When you're honest in the media people seem to think you're not vulnerable. It's the age of the instant, anonymous response, of online "trolls" and hate mail and petty cyber abuse. Everyone has an opinion, especially when it comes to anorexia or other people's weight. But even though the harsh stuff sticks with me, I'm learning not to take it to heart.

This morning, as I am thinking about pressures, an email from my editor arrives. She's in her early forties and hoping to have a baby too.

Just trying to get pregnant is stressful in itself—so many times over the last two years I was really down when my period came, especially if it was a bit late and I was hopeful. And then there were the awful feelings of jealousy and unfairness when other people got pregnant . . . The idea of combining those emotions with simultaneously trying to recover from anorexia—well, it must be a hell of a ride!

"A hell of a ride" is right. And I've probably gone about this all wrong, taking on too much, trying to solve all my problems at the same time, wanting immediate results and a perfect outcome (as anorexics always do). The urgent health priority, to recover from anorexia, has been getting all mixed up with the baby thing and the relationship thing and the independence thing. In a way they're separate issues—and in an ideal world I would address them one at a time—but the reality is less straightforward. And then there's me and Tom: a relationship that is, at times, fairly conflicted. We're both quite solitary souls, used to our own company—Tom endlessly traveling his lonely planet, me with my own weird struggles. The last few years have been very happy but also very volatile times. I used to think jealousy was a form of flattery—in other words, the more jealous someone is, the more he loves you—but now I know it's one of the most corrosive, pointless, destructive emotions. Jealousy reveals a lack of trust, not love, and it breeds paranoia, secrecy, and insecurity. None of us is perfect, and I wouldn't want to pretend that my relationship is either. Tom and I adore and torment each other in roughly equal measure. On top of that, as we're tentatively moving toward living together, we're also now trying to conceive, and I'm trying to beat a mental illness that has nothing and everything to do with pregnancy and relationships and babies and love. It hasn't been simple.

Sometimes everything in life happens at once: the good and the bad, love and conflict, all raining down from the skies.

* * *

I think it's worth mentioning these pressures, because they form the backdrop to this story. Perhaps they explain why everyone's advice of "Just relax, let yourself heal, look after your body, feed yourself; time will do the rest" has been almost impossible to follow.

My path to motherhood is no harder than for some other women, just different. I know of couples with "unexplained infertility" who try for years to conceive, at huge financial, emotional, and physical cost. While some people battle with polycystic ovaries, or low sperm count, or even just finding the right partner at the right time, I'm so aware that my own situation is largely self-inflicted. "But you're not infertile, just underweight" is simultaneously the most hopeful and frustrating piece of advice from my GP.

And I feel guilty for causing all this worry to others, and damage to myself. But I've kept going, and I suppose that shows strength. Despite what I've admitted about my shaky foundations and self-hatred, I must at some level have believed in myself to carry on when it looked hopeless. I haven't conceived, but I haven't really had the chance yet. Now that my period is back we can start trying for real.

This morning I cycled up to the drugstore and bought three boxes of their most expensive conception supplement—a present to myself! I felt idiotic, sort of furtive, like a teenage boy buying condoms, but the cashier didn't seem to notice. Obviously I've been taking folic acid for months, just in case, but this supplement is the real deal: it's called Mum-to-Be and shows an image of a woman cradling her massive baby-bump. Is any woman ever ready for the physical reality of pregnancy until it happens? The picture of that swollen stomach freaks me out.

* * *

"Things do not change; we change."
Henry David Thoreau

I never thought I'd change. Since the age of nineteen, I have dedicated myself to starvation. It's an unkind, destructive, pointless form of punishment. The psychologist who called anorexia "self-harm" was right. Now for the first time I am focusing on personal growth: Yes, I have grown; I take up more physical space in the world. Not only do I weigh 15 pounds more than I did at the start of this book, but I'm also an inch taller. I can't pretend to understand the science behind this, but it's true, I'm taller—and I know of other anorexics whose feet have increased a size as they've recovered! Perhaps it's just that everything gets proportionally larger with weight gain—as Dr. Robinson told me years ago, "there's just slightly more of you." And I'm fitter, not fatter: I cycle around town these days and every muscle in my body feels strong, not exhausted. Putting on weight is not pain-free, but there's something satisfying about having the confidence to accept that there is more of me. Nutrition is important now, for me and for a baby.

It's as though for the last fourteen years I refused to accept that I had needs and appetites like anyone else. It was a long process of waging war against my physical self, of detachment from my body. This will sound hopelessly "new-agey," but I am learning to reattach myself to this body, to live inside my body and nurture it, to "be" my body, not just a chaotic bunch of feelings and emotions inhabiting a physical shell. My body isn't just outside me, it *is* me.

During the last year, nothing much has changed in the wider world in terms of women and their bodies; if anything, the pressure has intensified. Today's *Daily Mail* reports:

> Adverts for a pro-anorexia t-shirt for young girls carrying the slogan "Nothing tastes as good as skinny feels" have been banned by the Advertising Standards Agency. The statement, controversially promoted by the model Kate Moss, has been condemned for fuelling eating disorders.
> (*Daily Mail*, 10 August 2011)

This headline takes me back to the start of my journey almost a year ago; only it's me who has changed, not society. The general obsession with celebrity culture increases, the cosmetic surgery industry flourishes, airbrushing of images continues, unsafe diets proliferate, and disordered eating, body dysmorphia, and self-hatred become the norm. Only last week there was a media flurry over reports that girls as young as five are being hospitalized with severe anorexia. The *Daily Mail* called it "a shocking illustration of how early they can become obsessed with body image," and commented, "in today's looks-obsessed society even the tiniest girls are internalizing media images that tell them . . . that thin equals perfect" (1 August 2011). Similar scare stories popped up in the media all summer—but we should keep the figures in context: a total of ninety-eight children in the U.K. between the ages of five and seven have received treatment in the last three years for eating disorders (*Daily Mail*, 9 September 2011). That's a tragedy for those families, but it is an infinitesimally small number in our population of 62 million (and there are reasons apart from anorexia why young children may struggle to eat). To me, of far greater concern is the explosion in childhood obesity; there are predictions that, if we carry on as we are, 90 percent of today's children could be overweight or obese by 2050 (NHS, *Help Stop Childhood Obesity Before It Starts*, 2011). The U.K. now has many, many more morbidly obese five-year-olds than severely underweight ones— and we shouldn't forget that being overweight as a child stores up even more long-term health problems than being underweight. Seventy percent of overweight eleven-year-olds go on to be obese young adults. Nonetheless, it seems that the sight of a very thin child still horrifies us more than the sight of a very fat child—as if we find overfeeding more acceptable than the look of starvation.

While society may be moving in the wrong direction, it looks like science is moving in the right direction. Among the inaccurate media sensationalism about eating disorders, some interesting research has started to emerge. A few days ago I was sent a pre-publication copy of the Ravello Profile, which is an international neuropsychological test investigating the cognitive profiles of people with eating disorders. The Ravello researchers have identified specific patterns in brain chemistry that may indicate a genetic predisposition to anorexia. Looking at the activity and functioning of the brains of those with eating disorders, they find that anorexia is "a diagnosable illness and not a behavior choice." In other words, the anorexic is not to blame, and nor are parents or the media. Earlier research has also highlighted neurological differences between anorexic and nonanorexic patients, and a significant degree of heritability. Johnson states that "anorexia, like schizophrenia, is a genetic disease . . . an individual is twelve times more likely to develop the disease if a relative has the illness" (Johnson, "Genetics Research: Why is it important to the field of eating disorders?" taken from www.eatingdisordershelpguide .com/genetics.html, 2006).

This research, although inconclusive, really matters. For too long eating disorders simply haven't qualified as serious diseases that merit funding and treatment. They have often been dismissed as faddy diets or food hang-ups; selfish, silly, female concerns. I can only repeat the statistic: up to 20 percent of anorexics will die from their condition. If that's not serious, then what is? There's no question we need more understanding of this complicated illness.

On a personal level, what difference do these findings make? Is it a relief to discover there's an "underlying malfunction" in my brain circuitry, that it's not my fault? Am I alarmed at the neurological findings, or do I feel vindicated? Does it help me come to terms with all that I've wasted, and lost, over the last fourteen years?

Oddly, not really. I've always sensed—however unscientifically—that something is broken inside my head. Now I know I'm not going crazy, that anorexia really is a brain disease. I never understood why most women can diet and exercise and not develop anorexia, whereas I did. It turns out there may be a reason after all.

I don't anticipate a miracle treatment for anorexia anytime soon. But honesty is a powerful weapon in fighting this condition, and I know that I've helped some people—fathers and daughters, sisters, even adult couples—to have those first conversations. An inpatient in her early thirties recently emailed me from an eating disorders clinic.

I just got married and am desperate to conceive a baby too. In the last six months my weight has plummeted and I'm now receiving professional help in hospital for the first time. Throughout this my husband has stood by me, struggling to understand the illness. Your column, in many respects, has been his education . . .

She ends:

And if you find the secret, from a purely selfish perspective, please don't keep it to yourself.

Of course I don't have the secret. Now that my period has come back, now that my BMI is healthy and my weight is higher, am I recovered? Not yet, no. But writing about anorexia has taken away some of my fear.

* * *

And yet, some fear remains: fear of food, fear of change, fear of commitment, fear of loving and being abandoned; more than anything, fear of life without anorexia. As illogical as it sounds, I'm waving goodbye to something that is a huge part of me. My life has revolved around this eating disorder for fourteen years now. I still shudder at the label "anorexic," but I can't deny that it's part of my identity. There's a sense of loss.

Before I leave it behind I've been trying to understand what it has meant to me. What was the significance of anorexia, an illness that has lasted nearly half my adult life? Despite destroying so much, did anorexia have any purpose? There is no question it held me back professionally—I missed so many career opportunities, unable to socialize or network in eating situations—and emotionally, I squandered countless relationships. The collateral damage of anorexia is incalculable: intimacy, honesty, peace of mind. But are there any positives?

I think there are. I'm a different person from who I was pre-anorexia. Before, my life was rather gilded; I had a tendency to take my health, my good fortune, even other people, for granted.

After, I'm quieter and more reflective; I've learned what it is to be alone, to be sad, to feel frightened. Before, I was surrounded by people; I was sociable, lively, but sometimes thoughtless. After, I have fewer but closer friends. The illness made me vulnerable but also more resilient.

Anorexia sent me to the dark side. And when you've been there—whether through depression, cancer, divorce, stroke, violence, injury, bereavement, pain, or trauma—you tend to look around you with renewed wonder at the world you nearly lost. It may be facile to say that those who have known suffering are kinder, better people, but on the whole I've found it's true.

So anorexia was not pointless. I refuse to believe I wasted the last fourteen years. I never had an actual nervous breakdown, but the gradual physical breakdown forced me to stop, to look inside myself, to admit that I was struggling, that I was lonely; finally, to ask for help. I found deep oceans of support and kindness I never knew existed in those closest to me. I came into contact with total strangers. I discovered a new kind of respect for my body and began to understand that it needs fuel and care in order to function properly. These last few months, in particular, on this slow road to recovery, I'm even learning to be patient. I can distinguish what matters—family, love, health—from what doesn't—ambition, success, appearance—in a way I couldn't before.

Nothing in life is wasted; everything is experience. Mental illness, too. In the oddest way, anorexia got me back in touch with myself. I can't pretend I would have chosen to take the path I took, but I think I'm finally getting to where I need to be. I remember that my dad used to tell us one of Leonard Woolf's sayings: "The journey not the arrival matters." I didn't understand it as a child, but I'm starting to now.

Chapter 16

As One Door Closes . . .

Sunrise over London, early autumn now. I find myself thinking back to that other dawn when I walked in the snow, sipping my coffee and eating that first momentous Kit Kat. It's less than a year ago and yet it feels like a lifetime. I'm standing on my balcony in cut-off shorts, pink flip-flops, and a white T-shirt, with a French-press of coffee. I woke a few hours ago, showered, and packed the last of the boxes. Now I'm waiting for Tom to arrive with the rental van. So am I scared? Excited? Yes and no, to both.

But that's OK. I'm starting to see that life isn't always black and white: it can be good and bad, perfect and imperfect, happy and sad, all at the same time. I'm starting to understand that most of us are just feeling our way through. We all have ups and downs—moments when we feel confident, moments when we feel like failures, fat days and downright sexy days, relationships that flounder, and secrets that shame us. No one has the instruction manual for life—how to feel, who to love, or what to do next. I'm trying to take it one day at a time.

There has been a lot of talk recently about seasonal confusion—it's been a really strange year for weather. Winter dragged on long into March, and then suddenly summer arrived in early spring. April was hot and dry, August was cold and rainy, and I feel as mixed-up as the seasons. Standing on the balcony I touch the bracelet on my left wrist and smile. "All shall be well, and all shall be well . . ."

This bracelet came into my life unexpectedly last week. I had returned from a long day's writing at the British Library to find a surprise waiting for me at home. A package on the doormat, and I didn't recognize the handwriting or the postmark. Curious, I opened it to find a delicate bracelet wrapped in fuchsia-pink silk.

With the bracelet there was a letter from a *Times* reader, explaining:

Although I've never been a sufferer of anorexia I have other obsessions, so I understand what you're going through. I love making jewelry, and some of the beads I use have supposed healing properties.

She went on to explain that these healing powers may be genuine, or they may be "mumbo-jumbo," but it helps if the wearer believes in them.

With this in mind, I have made you a bracelet to wear. I selected stones with a connection to fertility, stress, anxiety, compulsions, and insomnia as being of particular relevance.

She's certainly got my number! I held it up to the light, touching the strands of spun gold, fine beading, and luminescent stones. It fits perfectly, as if it was made for me. Well, it was.

There's mother-of-pearl "to calm and allay fears," and goldstone "for energy, courage, and positive attitude." Next is jade, an "emotional balancer and bringer of peace," and unakite, which "facilitates rebirthing and fertility." Agate "rebalances and harmonizes the body, heals the stomach, and uterus," and hematite "helps overcome addictions and enhances willpower." Last on my bracelet, and the prettiest stone of all, rose quartz "protects mother and baby, and purifies and opens the heart to promote self-love." Can a bracelet really have healing properties? Something about it makes me want to keep it near.

I hesitate there on the balcony with my coffee, postponing the inevitable. Inside, my flat is unrecognizable: clothes folded neatly in suitcases, books stacked in huge cardboard boxes, papers and documents in crates and folders, shoes jumbled up in trash bags. The bookshelves are naked, the closets are bare, and the fridge is empty (even by my standards). Everything looks a little dusty and sad. Tom will be here in less than an hour.

He's been going mad over in South London, preparing the flat for my arrival. Every time we've spoken he's been in the middle of another DIY job: dismantling an ugly old sofa to take down to the recycling depot, throwing out boxes of cassettes and videos, ripping the bathroom cabinet off the wall and assembling a new one with a door that doesn't fall off in your hands. He has cleared storage space for me in the loft, allocated half the closets for my clothes, and even changed the batteries in the smoke alarms. We've been an odd pair over the last few weeks, between our travels and hotel trips, me muttering about final chapters and trying to pack up my flat, and him attacking filing cabinets with hammers and mixing wallpaper paste.

And last weekend we finally found the desk. Not just any desk—we've been searching for this writing desk for two years. While we were reviewing a hotel near Cirencester, we drove into town for the afternoon and happened to wander into an antique shop. It was one of those cavernous warehouses that go on and on, rooms piled high with bric-a-brac, through courtyards and around corridors stuffed with old books and records and chairs and tables—and in an attic, at the top of a winding staircase, we found the desk. We both knew it instantly. It's old wood but not too old, three drawers to the left-hand side—a classic writer's desk, elegant but large enough for a computer and plenty of papers and cups of coffee—and the perfect size for my study. Within minutes, Tom and the antiques dealer were maneuvering it down the narrow stairs while I waited outside by the open car. They just managed to fit it in and we drove back to London the next day with the wooden legs jutting between us.

So now I even have a desk waiting for me in the new study. And yet it's a wrench leaving my flat. Whatever I've gone through—and the last four years have been some of the loneliest of my life—I've also been happy here. Contented, private, safe. Hours spent reading in bed, or soaking in the bath, or talking on the phone as I stretched out on the wooden floor. I gave up smoking here; I wrote many of the columns here, sitting at a high stool at the breakfast bar. I've sunbathed on the balcony; I've even had the occasional family party here, although I've never cooked what one might call a "meal" for a "guest." I sweated buckets one hot summer, up on a ladder, painting these ceilings and walls; I saved up for the new kitchen, which is still pristine. I've spent hundreds of nights in this bedroom. I'm not someone who can cast off places easily. This flat has become part of me.

But even as I'm feeling sad, torn between the past and the future, I know it's time. A well-known extract from Ecclesiastes (3:1) comes into my mind—I remember it because I read it at my grandmother's funeral: *"To every thing there is a season and a time to every purpose under the heaven. A time to be born and a time to die . . . A time to weep and a time to laugh; a time to mourn and a time to dance."*

* * *

And now is a time for change. I still haven't made sense of anorexia, and I'm still not sure what "recovery" means. I don't even know if it's behind me—yet. But I am beginning to understand myself a little more.

For example, the anxiety I've been feeling about moving is natural, normal. It's not about Tom, it's about me. Personal change is frightening but not impossible. Just like taking that first bite of Kit Kat, just like anyone who has ever stood at a crossroads, I have a choice right now. I can take the brave route, into the unknown, or I can chicken out and stick to what I know and lose everything: lose Tom, lose the chance of a baby and marriage and happiness. Every cell in my body is scared about this move, but I'm going to do it. I have been thinking about strategies for coping in tough times, and I wrote myself a list: *Radio 4, reading, writing, swimming, talking to my mum, seeing my family, eating lots of greens, drinking milk*. Simple, effective tactics to keep me sane, all of which I can do at Tom's. In between the fear I keep getting twinges of excitement. I'm going to live with my boyfriend. I really am.

The sun has risen high over the buildings opposite, warming my face and arms. It looks like another beautiful autumn day. As I pick up my coffee cup and turn to go inside, I hear the sound of tires crunching over the gravel in the courtyard below. I lean over the balcony and there's Tom, waving a bunch of white flowers at me from the window of a moving van. My heart leaps. Yes, it's time to go.

Acknowledgments

Many people have provided help and advice during the writing of this book. Particular thanks are due to the following:

To my agent, Sarah Such, for her support and guidance over the last few years. To all at Summersdale Publishers, especially Elly, Alastair, Suzanne, and Nicky, for their hard work on the book. Thank you to Justine Gore-Smith for copyediting and Abigail McMahon for proofreading, and to Robert Smith for the wonderful cover. Special thanks to my Summersdale editors Jennifer Barclay and Abbie Headon for their patience, editorial insight, and friendship.

Thanks to the many readers of *The Times* who have written and emailed over the past twelve months. Sometimes negative, usually positive, your support has been essential to this process of recovery. It's easy to read something and not bother to respond, so thanks to everyone who wrote to share their experiences and offer advice. Your generous, thoughtful messages keep me going. In particular: Hannah Joels, Raelene Sheppard, Trina Beckett, Valerie Janitch, Leila Razavi, Katie Butler, Toni Ross, Ceara Hayden, Deanne Jade, and Grace Bowman. A truly inspiring bunch of women—and now lifelong friends.

To Dr. Paul Robinson, Pramjit Kaur, and everyone at the Russell Unit, thank you for looking after me. I know it's taken me far too long to get to this point—but all your work was worthwhile. Both Dr. Robinson and my GP Dr. Richard Garlick deserve medals for their patience! Thanks to Mary George at Beat and Dr. Daghni Rajasingham for sound advice.

To my editors at *The Times*: Emma Tucker who gave me a break into journalism with a weekly column, Vanessa Jolly and Corinne Abrams—it's an absolute privilege to write for you. Thanks also to Lesley Thomas (who commissioned my first article), Nicola Jeal, Jane Knight, Laura Deeley, and Fiona McDonald-Smith at *The Times*. Thanks to Jane Garvey at *Woman's Hour*, to Stephen Nolan at Radio Five Live, Sam Baker and Brigid Moss at *Red*, and Kate Faithfull-Williams at *Grazia*.

The greatest thanks, of course, go to family and close friends. Anorexia is unpleasant for everyone, not just the sufferer, and you've all gone way beyond the limits of ordinary human kindness. Thanks to my godmother, Rita Guenigault, always ready with a smile and a large glass of wine. To TGW, in loving memory. To my friends Mark Walsh, Jo Kemp, Libby Courtice, Susan Archer, and my aunt Alison. To my best friend, Darren Bird, who always sneaks out of the office to cheer me up in Starbucks. To Tamsin Hickson, Aldo, Marianne, Keith, and all the Italian crew for the week in Mogliano when I was falling apart. To Beth Wilson and Michael Rose, in whose house and garden I wrote several chapters of this book.

How do you thank someone who introduced you to the love of your life? A million thanks to Leonora and Carolyn Bear for your matchmaking skills . . .

To my boyfriend, Tom (who gets an entire chapter of thanks and doesn't need any more here).

Thank you to my beautiful sisters, Katie and Alice, and my brothers, Philip and Trim. From childhood rivals to the very best of friends.

Finally, to Cecil and Jean Woolf, my amazing parents. It is not words could pay you what I owe.